The Darn Liberal Won't Shut Up

Letters and Essays
by
Naomi Silvertree

Naomi Silvertree

To order additional copies of this book, contact:
Naomi Silvertree
PO Box 5256
Arcata, Ca. 95518

Author's Foreword

These letters and essays have been written over the last twenty plus years. Some of the letters have been published in newspapers. Many of the later ones have not been since I don't presently have a lot of access to the internet and papers now prefer that one's writing simply be uploaded directly as it saves them much labor when one does so. Some of the letters will be outdated. I include them anyway since, except for details, it remains difficult to differentiate whether I am talking about Bush or Trump. Others, though written some years ago, remain timely as the situations and attitudes described remain fundamentally unchanged. I expect I am primarily preaching to the choir. For what it is worth, I present this work anyway. Whether you accept or reject my thinking and ideas, I hope they are at least informative and interesting, and perhaps even useful. Some of the letters would, for length, fit better into the category of essays but, since they are responses to letters written by others, I place them in the category of letters.

A friend of mine once told me I sound like an Old Testament prophet. I'm not sure whether that was a complement or an expression of scorn. It was apparently humorous at least. It is what it is.

Naomi Silvertree

Naomi Silvertree

Essays

OPENING THOUGHTS

One of the fundamental questions we must ask ourselves, whether or not we are parents, is what kind of world do we want for children. The answer will differ depending on individual backgrounds. Where can any of us begin in the creation of a world that is good for children except with ourselves? The crassness, cruelty, and mindlessness we all encounter is not going to be changed in anyone else. Walking the line between gullibility and cynicism in a balanced way never is easy. There's no prescription. Not only because each relationship is unique, but because the capacity of our own hearts for wise compassion or outrage at cumulative wounding is always in flux.

Religious values are uppermost in many minds as a remedy for what is seen as a disintegrating society and/or cultural war. Whether one's framework is religious or secular, if it does not truly address the heart, it cannot provide a solution. I hope we can believe in the essential goodness of the heart, however deeply it may be buried in some.

The will to harm springs from many sources:

Self-hatred or fear of elements in the self-projected onto others (racism, sexism); ignorance (fundamentalist religion); the mistaken belief inherent in the machismo and greed of our culture that power over others manifested in "winning" constitutes real power (much of the business world and, increasingly, the arts, and the relentless one-upmanship in so many relationships.)

The question becomes then, when striving to do our part to create a world that is good for children, how do we address the heart?

Love is being fully present with the person you are with and exploring spirit and sensuality together. It is open and direct expression and cherishing of affectionate tenderness. When we bring an attitude or an action to the world, we can ask ourselves if it cherishes the essential tenderness of the other's heart. We must also ask what is essential and tender in ourselves that the human process of being vulnerable needs to heal and we must proceed without self-delusion. Doing this, perhaps we can bring some nurturing to the world.

A world that is good for children will be a world that is good for adults as well, because the capacity for joy and creativity that is our birthright will not have been ruined by the process of becoming adults, but celebrated as the unfolding of our true and vital being.

Abortion

Feb. 7, 1995

Editor:

I would like to point out a simple fact regarding abortion that some antiabortionists are apparently ignorant of. To feel pain one must have synapses in the brain. A six week old fetus has no brain synapses and therefore cannot feel pain.

The abortion controversy is not really about the right to life. It is about keeping women in their place. A therapeutic abortion in a proper medical setting poses little risk to the pregnant woman. A back-alley-coat-hanger abortion certainly does.

We surround our young people with a popular culture that blares sex because it sells goods so effectively. We feed children sex hormones, that is growth hormones (that increase corporate profits) via meat and now milk, (BGH) and wonder why they are becoming sexually mature at 10. Then we tell them don't do IT when one of the greatest adolescent urges is to be part of the in-crowd, to either score or claim to have scored.

Girls also still get the very traditional cultural message that without a man's love they're not okay. Having a lover proves you're okay. They dream their dreams of sweet secure domesticity or, perhaps high adventure together as promised by many a glamorous ad. These are the same kind of ads that delude them into believing they're expressing their individuality when they become tobacco addicts like so many around them. Women give sex to get love just as men give love, or pretend to in order to score. I am tempted to say the so called sexual revolution changed all that. Men got what they always wanted, i.e. sex without responsibility, except that men have been impregnating and abandoning women for centuries. Women got blamed, labeled as whores, and stuck with the kid and still do, as if condoms haven't been around since the 1600's at least.

It has been said that the measure of a civilization is how it treats its women and children. Where are the supports that help women raise their babies to a good life if they are not to have abortions? Where is the education for women's self-esteem to teach young women they're okay as fundamental human beings even when they're not some hunk's trophy? In the U.S. we're willing to spend $2000 for the right to spend even more money on a season's football pass, but we can't afford homeless shelters that serve many women and children, many of whom are victims of domestic violence that statistically increases after the football games that promote ultimate machismo. We worship this brutality even though it is now well known that serious brain damage results from many concussions and that this too leads to domestic violence and other criminality. We want to cut food programs for the elderly and children to balance the budget, yet spend billions in tax dollars bailing out financiers and savings and loans depositors, even those with over $100 K, who tell the small folks we must be self-reliant, and trust in trickle down. Or should we call it tinkle down? Then we want to talk to our young people about values? Baloney.

Hunting I

October 27, 1995

Dear Editor:

I was outraged and disgusted to see hunters in the marsh right beside the bird sanctuary.

Most hunters hunt to prove to themselves that they are manly men, which is a bunch of crap in the first place. These guys can barely get beyond city limits. They have to hunt in an area where the birds are next thing to tame due to the proximity of the bird sanctuary where people walk every day.

It is despicable that people who are out murdering hapless, innocent wild creatures have, in their monstrous stupidity, not the slightest concept of the horror of what they are actually doing. They did not create these living creatures whose beauty and freedom represent nothing to them except an opportunity to be killers.

Anyone who can afford a gun, ammunition, and a hunting license can certainly afford food, so they are not hunting for survival by any means, but for decorations to be displayed in a glass case or crucified on a wall, there to gather dust.

Ambushing wild creatures who have little chance of escape and often will die a slow death due to maiming if they do, is ugly enough anywhere. It is totally disgusting next to a bird sanctuary.

Hunting II

12-06-95

Editor:

Well goodness, haven't I just stirred up a hornet's nest by daring to have an opinion that killing animals and birds for fun, i.e. sport, is unacceptable. Both letters I have seen against what I wrote proclaim justification of hunting by historic precedence.

You are right when you say I don't understand hunting. I fail to see how killing a beautiful living creature, especially without any genuine need, can be experienced as fun. Nor do I consider animal body parts hanging on a wall aesthetic, though I suppose they do have the advantage of not pooping on the sidewalk or wanting out at 3:00 a.m. They're dead after all.

Human beings throughout history have enjoyed nature without killing, so hunters have no monopoly on historic precedence in human choice on this issue. Where there is no real need, such as absolutely no other source of food, then preservation of life should take precedence. Now-a-days we have even more opportunity to, "keep their beauty with us forever." (Are you planning on angels dusting them in heaven, or are your grandchildren to be charged with this task?) We can support the preservation of our parks, (Yellowstone, for example, is being threatened by logging taking place outside its borders,) and wildlife refuges and sanctuaries and enjoyment of them without all the killing by enabling law enforcement to have enough manpower to stop poachers. I would far rather enjoy nature's quietude without guns blasting in the distance and encounter living creatures whose right to live I respect than hang a dead body part on the wall.

I don't kiss toads, by the way, I have more respect for them than to impose such a human custom on them, and sadly I haven't ever met one of those beautiful creatures around here. I did see some the size of desert plates on a visit to

Oregon and it was a real delight to watch and hear them plopping about.

There is a complaint regarding my failure to rant against McDonalds and Burger King. I don't patronize those institutions, nor do I patronize the meat counter of any store. People throughout history have chosen to live without flesh foods, so those who eat meat don't have a monopoly on this human choice historically either. Recent studies have shown that the longest lived people have next to no meat in their diets and some of our finest athletes today are vegetarians. There also seems to be a misunderstanding of my statement about "manly men" and hunting. I said most men hunt to prove to themselves (and others) that they are in this category. I didn't say I agreed with it. Nor would I claim that men have a monopoly on stupidity or cruelty. Anyone who internalizes machismo as the measure of their being, and some women do this too, perpetuates the dark and destructive side of human beings and I just think it's sad and wasteful when we have so much higher a potential.

Love of Guns

May 12, 1995

Editor:

I was briefly able, on the recent KHSU discussion, to point out that three out of three of the legitimate gun owners I happen to know have had guns stolen from them, either from their cars or their homes. I do not believe this is an isolated circumstance. Guns stolen from legal owners constitute a major resource for criminals seeking weapons.

The discussion, which I was unfortunately only able to listen to the last portion of, seemed to fall into the typical males for guns and females against guns.

Why are men so in love with guns? Establishing a position in one's social hierarchy, whether animal or human, takes precedence even over sexuality. For many people, especially the young boys who are taking guns into their schools, this is exactly what they are trying to do, get the most powerful position by having (being) the biggest gun. The relentless macho compulsion to be one up in any endeavor, or ability to control others through varying degrees of meanness (a trait not limited to males) and/or craziness so as not to be one down, is pretty much the bottom line of our culture. It is not what I would consider healthy, intelligent, or fulfilling our positive potential as human beings. Each of us helping each other to be the best we can be as creative, loving persons, not hierarchy and the concomitant bullying that embitters so many lives, especially of young people, needs to be our direction. I had that figured out by the time I was in 4th grade and took flak from my teachers for it.

What are some of the reasons touted for gun ownership? 1) Protection. I'm 45 years old and I'm no macho giant. I've been thoroughly disgusted by the macho bullies I've had to deal with all my life, but I never had to shoot any of them, though I can't say I wasn't mad enough to if I had owned a gun. 2) Protection of livestock. I have no argument with this, especially when so many people are irresponsible about controlling their dogs. 3) Hunting. Hunting in case of genuine need for food is reasonable. I haven't eaten meat since I was 16, however, so I know there is absolutely no need for meat in the diet. So why take the life of a wild animal when there is no need? Hunters maim or leave to a slow death as many animals as they kill. Killing for sport is killing to feel powerful. Preserving life and developing creativity constitute spiritual power, but too many people fail to realize this. 4) Eye/hand coordination (the same excuse used to legitimize violent video games.) You can get a lot more eye-hand coordination out of playing a musical instrument or painting a picture, and in the end with the latter activities, you have something that furthers civilization, not the same old phallic worship that now, on the grand scale, is destroying our planet.

RE: Rush Limbaugh

August 9, 1995

Editor:

Rush Limbaugh has a listener and viewership of 20 million people in seventeen half-hour shows per week of air time. Think of this next time he claims that his point of view is censored. His income was $18 million in 1984. Think of this next time he claims to be, "one of the little guys."

Many of his fans seem to see him as if he were a cult leader, some even to the point of issuing death threats against those who point out the real facts regarding his right wing campaign of misinformation. Others think he is merely funny. The only way this man is funny is if you share his prejudices. He claims to be "just an entertainer", yet Congress receives thousands of calls whenever he brings up an issue and conservative lawmakers daily brief him by phone and fax regarding issues on which they want him to mobilize pressure on Congress.

Who does Rush scapegoat? Is it corporate America,

that largely owns the media and their practices in lobbying campaigns, polluting, and their means of getting government contracts (which they somehow fail to refer to as "welfare")? Is it tobacco whose ads are inducing younger and younger children to get hooked on nicotine which will ultimately seriously impact the cost of health care in this nation? Is it the liquor industry that is just as dangerous to health as other drugs, producing, via fetal alcohol syndrome, many of the criminal behaviors we decry? Is it the ongoing nuclear/military industry that has already caused so much waste both in the economy and environment? No, it is women, the poor, environmentalists, and labor who are ridiculed and shut out. Why women? Because women know that what it takes to care for the children of this country is opposite of what it takes to maximize profits for corporations and the already fabulously rich, and because he has no respect for women. He brags about being fired from an early job for violating the music rotation by daily playing of the Rolling Stones' "Under My Thumb". The lyrics celebrate, "a girl who once had me down" but is now "a squirmy dog" who "just does what she's told." Women who want to call his show, he announced, should first send photos of themselves.

He says he's not a racist but his response to a caller stating that black people are 12 percent of the population and need to be heard was, "Who the hell cares." And, "They got a light rail system to East St. Louis where nobody goes?" (Radio 6/27/94) East St. Louis is home to 41,000 people, 98 percent of whom are African Americans.

Rush claims, "There are more American Indians alive today than there were when Columbus arrived." In fact, the pre-1492 population was 5 to 15 million. By the 19th century the native population was 250,000 and today fewer than 2 million claim Indian ancestry according to the Census Bureau.

Rush relies, not on scientists, but on Dixy Lee Ray for environmental information regarding CFCs, for example. She, in turn, relied on Rogelio Maduro, associate editor of a magazine produced by followers of Lyndon LaRouche, who believe that environmental protection is a genocidal plot masterminded by the Queen of England. Rush never debates because his so called facts would be shot down. Think about all this next time he claims to be incapable of lying.

The so-called Republican landslide was won with only 20 percent of the population voting. Ten years of propaganda and scapegoating led to the Holocaust. Look today at what Slobodan Milosevic has produced in Bosnia to see the power of the individual playing on prejudice. We now have a prison population that exceeds our university population in

California. We are building more prisons, criminalizing the poor, and gutting programs that provide a way out of poverty. The time for silence is past.

Humanocentric

Editor:

March 1, 1996

A few notes on current events.

Presently there is an attempt to clear John Salvi, the murderer of two receptionists at two women's health clinics, on the basis of an insanity plea. His murderous acts were based on religious fanaticism, which certainly can be considered a form of insanity, as any murder must ultimately be. However, to put things in some perspective, if someone as obviously bonkers as Jeffry Dahmer was considered sane enough to go to trial and be imprisoned, by what stretch of the imagination should John Salvi not also be?

I also note most of the defense of the proposed ballot measure to kill mountain lions is based on the premise that human needs and values are superior and must take precedence over other living creatures we share the planet with. I doubt there has been any great increase in mountain lion population. What is happening is twofold: 1) More and more humans are moving into outlying areas that are lion habitat and 2) lion habitat, with massive corporate clear cuts, is being destroyed on an unprecedented scale. They are running out of places to live in peace, as is wildlife worldwide. People's problems with increased numbers of deer munching down their yards are much the same except, of course, deer aren't carnivores. If humans weren't so single-minded about making the world safe for the cattle that they have no genuine need to eat, there could be a lot more harmony with the natural world.

Consider the fact that throughout human history people have been slaughtering each other en masse in war, razing each other's civilizations, torturing both humans and animals, enslaving each other, having crusades, the Inquisition, witch hunts, colonialism, lynching, genocides, vivisection, death camps, foot binding, unsterilized and unanesthetized clitorectomies and infibulation for the sake of maintaining a woman's virginity for the future husband who will feel like a real man only when he can rip her open; rape, child molestation, pornography, snuff films, serial killers, mass killers, and drug pushing. We presently are causing extinction of many species at unprecedented rates, polluting the environment to the point of no return, all for hierarchical greed, religious fanaticism, nationalism, sexism, racism, or some combination thereof.

The dominant paradigm of our culture is that one is either one up or one down. This hierarchy is maintained by daily bullying and back stabbing, not to mention the constant lying that goes on with the sole purpose of getting into somebody's pants. So what's so wonderful about humanity that we should take such precedence? We have opposeable thumbs, build cathedrals and write symphonies? Hold the real horror of what we are for but a moment and know our glories are less than dust. If we truly want young people to have a future, we must indeed become moral beings as we have rarely been before, and not a morality of religious fanaticism, but a morality of genuine love and respect for all of life that humanocentrism, cannot inform any more than sexism or racism can.

Work Ethics

November 4, 1996

This is in response to a letter of October 29 regarding work ethics.

Without doubt, having a work ethic and ethical standards about one's work is essential. It would be wonderful if having these good qualities produced the kind of control over one's life we would all like to have. If it did, I would certainly now be well established in the field of medical transcription.

I did many of the things that the above mentioned letter recommends. I continued my education making every effort to learn new vocabulary. I was rarely late and called in sick but once on my last job, which lasted 14 months, and not at all on the others. I was well groomed in any situation where I would be seen by the public.

In four years I quit one job and was fired from three. Let's see why.

After getting my medical secretarial certification from College of The Redwoods, I worked in what could be described as a sweat shop, learning more about medical transcription because I realized I did not have the gregarious, extroverted personality best suited for work with the public. I was consistently overlooked for promotion to any new skill areas, even after I completed the two semester HROP medical transcription course. Taking that course required a two hour round trip commute five days a week. I went to school in the morning and worked the afternoon and evening, as I had been requested to on my hiring.

The sole purpose of never allowing me to go into new skill areas was to make sure I would not get enough hours to qualify for the health insurance that was falsely promised me and reneged upon four times. Every day for a year I'd call in to see if there was work and was guaranteed nothing. I was paid by the page. When the health insurance charade finally forced my employer to cover one person, and the provider said that even though I was a couple of hours short it would really be enough for me to be eligible, I asked again about my coverage, quoting him regarding the adequacy of my hours. "Well, something might happen to your hours," my employer replied in a huff, not even looking at me. Oh, yeah. Duh. Well, I finally got it that I was being totally squirreled around. How her case went when she got into trouble for not turning in her workman's comp money I have no idea.

My next job doing radiology reports lasted six months. The doctors were not happy with me the first three months, and rightfully so. Radiology has a big vocabulary and was a specialization I had not gotten in my course. I learned it on the job which was weekends. I arrived promptly at 8:00 a.m. The problem probably came when the person who trained me one of these days who, because of my hiring, had been put onto new material that was difficult for her, wanted to leave promptly at 4:00 and I didn't mind staying on a bit to make sure I got things right. I no longer needed her there, but that didn't seem to register with her. If looks could kill, three minutes after 4:00 I'd have been dead.

I was told by the 22 year old office manager (I was 46) that I should now do ten reports rather than the seven reports I was successfully (though barely) doing per hour and I would have two weeks to get up to speed. The best transcriptionist of the lot of us (the only one who considered it her genuine profession) had said seven in an hour was an adequate goal. I was fired though it had been three months since I had gotten a report back with mistakes to correct. "Have you considered marketing your art?" he asks as I am blowing snot into my hands. Right.

On my next job I also worked six months with no complaints from the doctors regarding either the quality or quantity of my work. Then we got a new head transcriptionist who cheerily proclaimed, "I've got 25 years of experience. Ask me any questions you like." So I did, and she told the head of the clinic she couldn't work with me because I asked too many questions! Fired again. What a set up. This after she had looked doubtful and wondered if she too should take any courses in transcription, as I had, since she had never had any. I heard they were lovers, so I guess that didn't help my case either.

My final job in the transcription field lasted fourteen months. On the last six months of this job I was scapegoated for one thing after another. For instance, losing reports though it was my supervisor's desk that looked like Godzilla's hidey hole, behind which I found two-week-old unmailed letters among the great pile of papers that had gotten shoved of the back of her desk. (I had been looking for an electrical outlet when I discovered this mess.) When I denied the accusations, I was demeaned as defensive and unwilling to deal with the issues. Am I supposed to admit mistakes I didn't make? The answer must be yes, if your supervisor is the mother of a dear friend of the doctors.

I kept working even though I was being treated like a liar. Finally she told me to look for another job though I had faithfully come in whether they had five minutes or three hours of dictation, and even on three occasions when they had none but didn't bother to tell me. Then there was the time she changed the size of the font and left a note to another member of the crew telling her to have fun with the font sizes, then did not change it back to normal size. It really screwed me up because I had never been taught how to deal with that aspect of computers. In my four years of working these jobs my typing speed improved from 52 to 63 words per minute. I asked for a letter of recommendation from the doctors, with whom I was on good terms, and eventually got one though this supervisor tried to prevent that.

This did not end my attempts to find a field of work different from the many years of following in my mother's footsteps cleaning houses. I enrolled in a program that essentially provided free labor to non-profits with the aim of giving a person experience in various job fields (since defunct.)

So I tried to become a store clerk. What can you really do with a bachelor's degree in theater arts, after all—especially when the major was chosen because I got out of high school convinced by my counselor and teachers that I was a genuinely stupid person (mostly because of my stance against the Viet Nam war and, since I was a math dunce, I was never permitted to take any science classes except the state-required biology class, which consisted of the fundamentalist Christian teacher reading <u>The Cross and The Switchblade</u> to us.) When I felt I was failing as a music major, I was told by a fellow college student that even a stupid person could get a degree in theater arts, so that's how I became a theater major. (I have some more positive ideas about that now, but that is a different story.) This is the story of my experience in this program.

There is a new volunteer. The first thing she says to me is, "I was beat up and my car was smashed in Tennessee."

I reply, with concern, "Why did they do that?"

She replies, angrily, "Are you blaming me for what they did?"

"No," I say. "I just wanted to know what was in their minds."

End of conversation. Most of the day when we cross paths she has a glassy stare and will not look at me. K. . . tells me she started a conversation with her in the same manner–apparently inviting comment about her pregnancy, then becoming hostile over a normal conversational question in reply.

Later I am making my second attempt on the cash register which is even more disastrous than the first. I concentrate very hard on getting the right numbers and buttons and once again am startled when the cash drawer hits me in the stomach, and equally startled when it buzzes loudly because I've entered a second number without first pushing a category button. The first day I did this customers laughed and I was instructed. But today no one was helping me and two very crabby ladies got very angry with me. The pregnant paranoid schizophrenic (above mentioned) sat beside me and started laughing.

It began thus–I was handed first a skirt with a pink tag but the price was torn off. I did not know what to charge because pink tags are individually (and higher) priced items. So I went to C. . . in the office. She said the tag had been torn off and asked if the customers were reputable people.

"I don't know," I said. She priced it at $6.95 and they then refused to buy it. Then they handed me a second skirt with no tag at all, so I did not know which rack it had been taken off of so I hung it up. They insisted they wanted it and it was off the other (blue tag) rack. So I said okay, $2.95 and rang that up. Meanwhile people are lining up behind them. You're new aren't you? The woman says. Yes, I'm an Experience Works Volunteer. I finally manage to ring up $24 or $25 in purchases. They hand me $25 and I give them the .85 change the machine says I owe them, but then I see I have been handed five not four ones and think I need to give them back one dollar which I do. Then I got really confused about the .85 thinking I had forgotten the tax and asked for the $1.00 back. (Which was of course ridiculous but I didn't want the till to be wrong.) "Get us one of those women back there. We want another clerk. Ask one of them to come up here. This one (meaning me) can't do this and that one thinks it is hilarious. SHE'S DEALING WITH PEOPLE'S MONEY!" "I like to laugh." says D. . . I leave the machine nearly in tears. D. . . dives on the cash register. "I'm an artist," I say, going back to the two women who have been fussing through the whole conversation with objects in the display cabinet behind the counter. "I was in the 14th percentile in math. They wouldn't even let me take science classes because I couldn't do algebra." Back then there was no such thing as tutoring, mentoring, or remediation. Because of my experience in high school, I got to college thinking there was no such thing as help, which is why I gave up on my first love, music. (Math was a very bitter point with me because I figured if I had been able to go into the sciences I might not have spent my entire life in poverty and washing toilets. I had always been really happy and excited whenever, in grade school, they handed out the shiny new science books. Well, I got thrown out of algebra on the first day because I couldn't understand the teacher's answer to my question. The kids that did get it looked at me like I was the biggest pain in the butt on the planet, which maybe I was—at least in algebra class on the first day.) One of the women then took over the register and the other mollifies the angry customer. They leave. I am invited to bag. I have success. The word "assholes." escapes my mouth however. "Well, Naomi's not afraid to say what she thinks," says the next customer in line with a somewhat horrified look on her face.

Friday, January 12

I come in on time at 10:15 and say good morning to D. . . Glassy stare, no reply. Well, whatever, I think. Shortly after this I see D. . . leaving. I am asked to Swiffer the floor which I begin to do, though there are several interruptions of the gofer nature. I am trying really hard to finish this because I know there are a lot of clothes to sort when I hear a conversation about something having been stolen. I move toward them and ask, "Something was stolen? What was it?" No one replies so I go back to my job. I hear more conversation, however. C. . . saying, "She came to me and said everyone was looking at her weird so I said, well these are our regular people and if you can't get along with them then you had better leave. I don't need any volunteers like that." And I hear the name of my friend K. . . and C. . .says "K. . . would never. K. . . is wonderful." Then I hear my name and C. . . says, "SHE'S THE NEXT ONE OUT OF HERE." I didn't think about it I was concentrating on my work so hard. I was told to take out the trash and did that. I sorted and tagged and got two racks of winter clothes out on the floor and went home, the arthritis pain in the base of my thumb acute after pinching God knows how many tags. Then I thought about it. It turned out they think D. . . stole an $80 bracelet.

Monday, January 15

I called C. . . and tell her I'd be in to have her sign my time sheet but I figured she doesn't want me there and tell her what I heard. She insisted she never said anything like that, doesn't even remember it. She would never say anything like that about me. "Everyone thinks you're wonderful. We're really glad to have you here. You must have heard something out of context. Thursday and Friday were really hectic. I was in and out of meetings. You haven't said anything to A. . . about this have you?" "No." I replied. She called me back and said she must have been having two conversations at once and was talking about scheduling volunteers, when they were leaving for the day. It was still morning and no one was leaving.

Frankly I doubted this, but I let her pretend to it so she could save face. I was making my own work arrangements and I went, even though it was not a real job but more of piecing things together as I have always done. I have told them to let me know what times they want me for 10 hours at the museum. I went to that even though I would not be paid. At least I'd be learning something.

We were permitted three positions in the program before we were considered as having used up our quota of learning experience. My final position was helping a senior program in Trinidad, where I lived. Asked to set up chairs for a weekly program, I did so but because my back was out I wore my brace and carried only two chairs at a time. This was considered too slow. I explained that my back was out from years of cleaning houses—stupidly indeed, all the high falls I had done in Aikido in my hope of becoming a women's self-defense instructor didn't enter my mind—and was angrily and contemptuously accused of being a cheater and a fake in order to get government money, which people of my ilk clearly had no right to, even though _they_ were benefiting from my government-paid free labor which they were glad to do. So, I gave them notice and that was that.

So you see, Mr. B., there are other factors, like office politics, classism, and down-sizing, over which the individual has no control, though corporations are more than happy to let the individual self-destruct out of guilt and a sense of failure, such as your letter promotes, that losing a job can produce. No matter how good we try to be, we can still get it in the neck. This is no excuse for abandoning one's work ethics. I haven't. I apply them to the field I worked in before my back went out, which led to my efforts to get into something less strenuous; namely house cleaning, and by which, along with a small inheritance, I earned my degrees. The pay is better and I am definitely more appreciated.

<u>Update 2017</u>

I now hold a Masters in Humanities and hope, since I am finally retired after 52 years of paying most of my own Social Security, and getting a little CalPers from seven and a half years as a high school Life Skills aide (which saved me from the bulb farm, where I was also an irritant since I didn't have the heart to slap the daffodils around and so increase my speed), to do something positive with my real creative skills, though making much of a living in a depressed North Coast economy was never to be among them.

Foibles

08-11-98

Editor:

The foibles of we humans continue to be sad and amazing. No age or gender has a monopoly on either wisdom or stupidity. Everybody has their own talents, capacities, and weaknesses. We all have to put one foot after the other anyway.

Injustice can be large or small, corporate or individual. American companies introduce terminator genes into seeds used to produce third-world food crops. This insures that, in the sacred name of commerce, farmers will be unable to produce their own seed because it will thus have been rendered sterile, forcing them into the ongoing purchase of seed from these companies, who often patent the plants these farmers have developed over centuries in the first place. They must purchase such seed, not only to produce a crop, but because the World Bank refuses improvement loans for such projects as schools and health clinics unless they do. Then we turn around and ask, "Why doest thou so?" when our embassies get bombed. Nothing like a little monopoly, greed, and self-delusion to insure the survival of the "fittest."

On a more intimate scale, relationships between men and women continue to be largely ridiculous. Both men and women separate their sexuality from their affections and treat each other as objects. Such separation is an effort at control. It is part of living in what Anne Schaef calls an addictive culture.

I would like to suggest that in any relationship companionship is the exchange for companionship, the only service we owe each other is a compassionate and vigilant honesty that enables us to own our processes, perceptions, and projections. Children should be brought in, not to serve our old age, but to be the best they can be for the whole of humanity and themselves.

Balance is always dynamic, teetering, vulnerable, dangerous, curious; sometimes full of grace, sometimes desperate. Vigilant honesty is the requirement for human progress in both the large and small picture.

Bible Path

July 21, 1999

I see a number of recent letters tout the Bible and the Ten Commandments as the arbiters of absolute truth and the solution to our moral problems. It is unfortunate that so many people completely misunderstand the Bible and see it in such monolithic terms.

There is a commandment, for instance, that says honor your parents, as parents should be for taking on the big and important job of raising children. But how many parents really are capable of doing more for their kids than fulfilling their own biological and sociological destiny? How do you honor a parent who beats his wife in front of his child and then beats his child? How do you honor a parent who does not, or cannot, protect her children from abuse? The Bible has a lot of wisdom, but it is not perfect. Like it or not, it is just as human a product as any other holy book, sociological or psychological theory, or historical writing.

Many believe in the Biblical proverb, "Spare the rod and spoil the child." Up to 50 percent, in a recent poll, now want to reinstate corporeal punishment in schools. If this maxim were really true, Hitler should have been the perfect human being as he was regularly beaten by his father. Is there something wrong with this picture?

Parents, often as not, pass on the abuse they themselves experienced as children. Yes, it can go the other way as people sometimes overcompensate with their kids for what they didn't get themselves. There are no formulas except education, love and presence and communication; being here now, alert to the reality of kid's lives and needs for balance. Parents aren't the only factor. We all struggle in an economy and culture that measures human worth by flashy possessions rather than by their joy, generosity, and creativity. If kids have the self-worth generated by honoring these aspects of their spirits, they aren't likely to shoot somebody for dissing their tennis shoes. Nor are they going to need to be controlled as if they were monsters.

Campus Smoking

11-6-99

Editor:

I am a returning student. I was last a student on this campus in 1988. Little has changed except one sad thing. When I was here nine years ago, no one was smoking. Now I can't go anywhere without winding up down-wind from the stink. It wafts into the building where we are trying to sing. A conversation about gardening begins with a bright, lovely young woman and I have to tell her to go away because she's taking out a cigarette at the same time.

Why young people begin to smoke in spite of having the knowledge that my parent's generation didn't have regarding health consequences, I assume, has to do with social pressure to look "cool" and ends with the same reason my mother didn't quit even though she was dying of emphysema, namely addiction. I know quitting isn't easy. In a study done with prisoners who were cocaine users, they received a concentrated form of nicotine (this substance is also used as an insecticide, by the way) and they believed they were actually getting cocaine.

I've seen addicts picking butts up out of the gutters. I've seen a young woman panting for breath at the top of the stairs who was yet unable to admit that this had anything to do with her smoking.   I've the globs of spit on the ground with coagulated stuff that looked like peanut butter. In fact, I stepped in that on this campus this summer at the bus stop. No one wants to admit that they're addicted to something, and to quit you have to begin with wanting to quit. But people do actually succeed in this and there is medical help and support groups available.

I know as you trot about striking your "cool" poses you probably couldn't care less about an uncool old fuddy-duddy who thinks your glamorous poses are pitiful. You have not cared about health hazards that are well-established facts. You have never helplessly watched a loved one go through the panic of a bronchospasm, a condition of emphysema where the lungs freeze up and you can neither inhale nor exhale. Other people have allergies that can be severely affected by tobacco smoke, inescapably blowing everywhere. In the ultimate human quest for glamor and the "right" to "pleasure" you're "cool."

Nonetheless, here comes the lecture about one more thing for you to think about. One third of the human race is infected with tuberculosis. Yes, right here in Humboldt County people do have this disease, not just in far off India. Many of the new strains are drug resistant. TB is making a come-back even in the U.S. Share a cigarette, or accidentally pick up the wrong cigarette out of a shared ash tray (of course for many of you the planet is your ash tray) and you've got it if the other smoker has it. You're in college now. You're supposed to have a genuine capacity for thinking. Prove it. Quit smoking.

Reflections On a Radio Discussion of Karma

September 2, 2001

The radio show guest spoke about karma. I neither accept nor reject the traditional "New Age" (circa 1850 courtesy of Helena Blavatsky) explanations of many of the mysteries that are part of our world—from UFOs, ghosts, telepathy, precognition in dreams, invisible teachers, negative energy cording, past-life recall, and apparent evidence of reincarnation. I have experienced these things, so I accept them as real, but cannot be dogmatic about how they should be explained. My father was into metaphysics, UFOs, Rosicrucians, Theosophy, Cabala, and heaven knows what else, so I grew up with so-called New Age concepts long before they became popular in the 60s. I offer this background to show I am no materialist skeptic in my rejection of the popular concept of karma as an explanation of so much of the human condition.

Karma is a difficult subject, but important since so many people believe in it. It seems to me, as a person who has lived in poverty all my life, is on medication for depression, who grew up physically and emotionally abused, as I did, that the idea that the universe always "balances" itself, and every so-called piece of bad fortune is a lesson we have either chosen to experience or been in need of learning, is a rather upper class luxury. It certainly brings comfort to those who already have comfort and takes the edge of any need for action for social justice.

While the accusatory, "You did this to yourself," or "You chose this," definitely can have psychological truth since we all have blind spots, it cannot be a full explanation for historical conditions, cultural outlook, psychological (familial) dynamics, (including addictions) or genetic manifestations of unbalanced brain chemistry and recessive genes. The fact that we are able to call upon imagination and spiritual (inner) resources to glean positive lessons from misfortune (the quadriplegic with MS decides she needed to learn to be still; the woman driven from her home by a paranoid, bipolar neighbor's relentless harassment decides that the experience of moving successfully can give her courage to move yet further in her life) is a tribute to human imagination and spiritual resources, not evidence of "chosen" karmic lessons that is frequently used to let perpetrators off the hook. That borders on superstition as much as the medieval belief that you could cure lameness in a horse by putting magic ointment on its shoes that were not even on its feet. Give the horse a two-month rest and, see, the ointment worked.

The universe is billions of years old. We are microbes on a grain of sand (if that.) Holiness is a felt reality in this place of storm light, hills, trees, seasons, silver dew on grass, rainbows over the sea, and sweet innocence. Then there is the utter horror of the dead child's gouged out eyes. Did that child choose to be born in a slum to a teen mother, whose culture teaches her she has no worth but in her ability to attract male attention (read redemption), where he would wind up on the streets and see too much? What karmic lesson is a mutilated cat, who yet struggled home, supposed to learn about human projection of hatred of the feminine onto it? Shall we accept from both the Ultra-Orthodox and the anti-Semite that the Holocaust was karmic punishment of sin? I don't think so.

Knowing the oneness of Divinity, and the dynamic unity of Divine and human blessing, one must live daily crucified on this cross of paradox. I have no answer but that each of us must persevere in manifesting whatever goodness (large or small) and growth we can muster, and live with the Mystery. We cannot blame any one thing for either good or bad fortune, including karma, whatever the psychological security need that may meet. There are too many dynamics in the web of the universe for that. Rather let us strive to see as clearly as possible what those dynamics are, own what is ours, and let the rest go, with blessing if possible.

Attack on New York

September 14, 2001

Editor:

While the attacks on New York and Washington were reprehensible and deeply saddening, as any act of violence is, they are understandable and not without cause. The United States is not the innocent victim of monsters who simply hate our life style and freedom. We have been bombing Arab countries for years. All over the world our operatives have assassinated democratically elected leaders and set up dictators who torture and repress their people.

Fifty years of tit for tat between Israelis and Palestinians has achieved nothing but deepening hatred and continued death and maiming of innocents, children, on both sides.

The first and only response of the United States to the present situation has been more of the same old macho garbage that created all of these situations in the first place. The world and its peoples and resources do not exist solely for the enrichment of Americans so we can have one more strip mall and maintain our standard of global warming. The U.S. has ignored major treaties and failed to put resources into perfectly viable alternatives for both transport and the economy because it would change a status quo that relentlessly funnels money to the "one percent."

It is injustice that breeds chaos. The belief in winning at all costs instead of listening permeates our culture and produces injustice and violence. With our culture of addiction, false entitlement, and violence as entertainment, how hard was it for people to realize they were seeing a horrible reality on September 11th and not another disaster flick? Can we learn to live without the impermeable denial that we are anything but heroes?

Bombing Afghanistan will only produce what violence always produces, more hatred, more excuses for the sickness of vengeful minds, more ecological disaster, the death of more innocents. It will solve nothing.

Fundamentalism

September 29, 2001

Fundamentalists of every stripe have one thing in common. They see the world in black and white. Living with the profound ambiguities of reality can be a place of great pain. It is far easier to demonize those we may see as corrupt or evil than to listen and try to understand complexity. This is not to deny the existence of corruption and evil, but the more we treat anyone as an enemy, the more they will tend to act like it.

There are indeed those who have deep mental illness that no amount of rationality can convert, no amount of kindness can transform. Hate is a form of mental illness, but abuse begets abuse. We must strive to rationality and kindness whether or not it always is effective. The alternative is magnification of evil and chaos.

All people of faith, as well as those of secular outlook, must turn away from seeing in black and white and from seeing as literal that which is poetic metaphor.

Acknowledging the failures of American foreign policy must not be written off as self-flagellation. It is a rational and mature step in the ongoing vigilance essential to the survival of democracy.

"Winning In Viet Nam?"

January 3, 2002   Editor:

I stand amazed and disgusted having run into someone who still believes we could have "won" in Viet Nam. Undoubtedly there are more yahoos out there, so I'll demand to know how many more children would you deform with napalm, how many more limbs blow off with land mines, how much more forest defoliate, how much more farm land poison out of production, how many more soldiers drive mad with training that attempts to turn them into heartless killers, how many more alcohol and drug addicted homeless vets, how many more agent orange cancers, how many more CIA abandoned armies and their families on welfare in Eureka, for U.S. to be glorious winners? What does this word mean, "win?" That the yahoos get to strut around with their nether parts erect, doing whatever they please? Well, Bronx cheer.

The only winners in war are the arms dealers and the multinational financiers that create the war machines of the

Hitlers, the Saddams, and the Ben Ladins as proxies in their war to make the world safe for oil and arms profiteering.

Universal soldier. You know the rest of the song.

American Dream

April 30, 2003 (with minor 2017 updated references)

Editor:

What is the American dream? Wouldn't most agree it means a country where basic human needs are met, a home where you can safely raise a family, a chance to earn a decent living, get an education, contribute to one's community, express generosity, experience simple joy in the garden or at the beach? We expect our democracy to produce this idyll, though I would not have been able to articulate it in those terms when, as a young person, my eyes would fill with tears when singing America the Beautiful. (For that matter, they still do.)

The American Dream of democracy has never been entirely real, but even what we did achieve was too much for the latest generation of Robber Barons like the Koch brothers, who dash every hope of the common people while lining their own pockets with off-shore tax havens and pushing the use of the use of coal and oil that is destroying the climate. Thus, achieving an education without a mountain of debt, housing, health care, and retirement are increasingly out of reach.

When Saddam Hussein was gassing his people he was our ally, whom we armed to fight a proxy war with Iranian fundamentalists. There would never have been a fundamentalist government in Iran if the CIA hadn't toppled their democratically elected government because they nationalized their oil fields, taking them out of British and American hands. The American-backed Shah and SAVAK, the Shah's secret police, (read torturers) replaced Iranian democracy. It's of course easier to get good business deals with strongman type puppet dictators. We aren't supposed to have this kind of historical memory. If we do, we are castigated as unpatriotic.

For every young person who dreams of a cottage with roses around the door, another fantasizes Valhalla where you "heroically" spend your day in slaughter, then come back to life and feasting at night, then do it all again the next day. Unfortunately they usually don't grasp that everyone in Valhalla is dead.

One billion people on this planet do not have access to clean water. Hello?

Four More Years

Editor:

Four more years. Abu Ghraib. Lies about WMD. Four more years. Lies about Saddam Hussein-Al Quaida-9/11 connection. Four more years. One hundred thousand dead Iraqi civilians, 1000 dead U.S soldiers. Four more years. Tax cuts for the richest one percent of Americans while soldier's families survive on food stamps. Depleted uranium weapons and the planned development of a new generation of nuclear weapons exposing U.S. Soldiers and the victims of our bombing alike, to radiation, resulting in cancers and birth defects. Four more years. The militarization of space. Billions for war, mountains of debt and economic draft for students. Four more years of black and white thinking, denial of the facts of history, attack on our civil liberties, denial of due process, disenfranchisement of legitimate voters. Four more years. Missile strikes against foreign journalists, radicalization of the entire world against whom, by this election, we have declared war. Four more years. Disappearance of 30 acres of unguarded explosives, now probably in use against American troops. Four more years of war profiteering and depleting public services. For more years of fundamentalist superstition that pushing Armageddon is equivalent to salvation. As a religious person myself, I can only pray that this mad manipulation of fear, of bombing the world into submission, can somehow be turned around before Armageddon is indeed created. Because there will be no salvation from such absolute denial of genuine spiritual values that honor life and cherish this planet.

Our World

January 14, 2004

Editor:

Our world is racked by horror and grief. Our culture, our history, is layer upon layer, generation after generation of grief. Who to scapegoat, who to blame, who to hate, who to punish; forever. As long as there is hierarchy, bullying, exploitation, mocking contempt of the humanity of others, and false beliefs, it will be forever. Given American hubris in the deployment of depleted uranium weapons and sale of WMDs to folks like former ally Saddam Hussein, our forever may not be so long.

Culture instills many unexamined false beliefs. If there is to be any hope of changing the human condition, we must examine the cultural and historical lies upon which the will to harm is based. But, like addicts deep in our disease, we live in denial.

Some deny the Holocaust and perpetuate the PTSD

trauma experienced by the Jewish people. Both the right and the left have been anti-Semitic, a stance easily taken in a culture that, even while proclaiming itself secular, has been taught from the time of Roman co-option of Christianity (see <u>Constantine's Sword</u> by James Carroll) that Jews were Christ killers. Others say, "Israel right or wrong" just as Americans in the Viet Nam era said, "America right or wrong."

Eighty five percent of both Palestinians and Jews want peace and accept the two-state solution. While it cannot be forgotten that Palestinians denied Jews refuge during the Holocaust because they falsely believed them to be agents of British colonialism, this cannot be redressed by the razing of houses and orchards or the building of fences. Neither can the latter be redressed by suicide bombings.

Take Back The Night
Editor:

Last night we had an important and cathartic yearly event--Take Back The Night. Many women, including myself, came forward and told the stories of how they survived abuse and molestation in their families. One thing marred the night for me. Though all of the grief of so many, and the gut realization that the pervasiveness of abuse is ignored by our society because it is the underbelly of our woman-hating culture is hard to bear, I do live with that every day. The mar for me was the inclusion on the table of a pamphlet that tried to proclaim and explain differences between S & M and abuse. I am not so much against the freedom of speech as the stupidity it implies. If there really was any difference, promoters of this inane crap wouldn't have to constantly claim there is.

Real love is being fully present with the person you're with and exploring sensuality and spirit together. It is open and direct expression and cherishing of affectionate tenderness, desire, and appreciation. It is not acting out some fantasy of power through abuse, nor the passive relinquishment of responsibility for sexual activity because your sexuality is buried under a load of guilt. That is what many parent-child relationships create. S & M is not love, it's repetition compulsion. Read Alice Miller's <u>For Your Own Good</u> to get a deeper understanding of this. S & M as rebellion is on a par with smoking. The ultimate S & M draws blood and kills. No one's inability to have an erection or be orgasmic is an excuse for abuse. Anyone who cannot experience their sexuality without needing to power trip or hurt their partner, or, let us be generous and say "fantasize" about hurting their partner, had better face the fact that they are damn sick.

Whether it is fantasy "play" or acting out of rage, it is only our culture ritualized, not only in the inherent abuse (it is okay to "hit, choke, slap, hurt" <u>inside</u> the context of a scene) but in the denial of responsibility inherent in our rape culture i.e. it's okay to rape and abuse, "they were asking for it."

Acting out of rage and guilt does not permit growth. It merely habituates rage and guilt and reduces relationships to mutual persecution. It is the wars of the nations on an individualized level. We need to have an enemy we can hate without guilt because we carry unowned, amorphous rage. Right now it's the Serbs, even as they in turn act out their rage over the abuse they experienced as victims of the Nazis and their Croat allies. Some may even want to be hated as yet another layer of excuse for the expression of their own rage.

All in all, I guess it's easier to wait for the Messiah than to deal with all the layers of self-deception and rage. Tell you what, folks. Nobody is going to do this work for us. We are the Messiah.

A Reply

August 16, 2004

Dear Mr. Flower,

I usually enjoy listening to Thursday Night Talk as you have articulate guests and important topics most of the time. I admittedly tuned I late last week to your show on the 12th but I did not have to listen long to realize the topic was completely disgusting bullshit, at which point I continued to listen briefly in the hope that something intelligent might yet be uttered. Nothing was so I turned it off.

It is some years now since I was a reentry student at HSU and was thus able to get the enclosed letter published in the Lumberjack. (See above.) I was informed about a year later that the Matrix had reprinted it with an article by someone who refuted me. I never saw that refutation, however, and as far as I am concerned there can be none. I am really sorry to see young people confused by the promotion of this narcissistic crap. Anyone, young or old, deluded into believing that S & M is "cool" is just pitiful. I suppose anyone who believes in tenderness, affection, and honor between human beings actually being consistently expressed as such (regardless of gender) is just an "ol' uptight", as I would undoubtedly be characterized.

S&M is crap and the people who promote it are deluded (at best) bullshitters and I don't need some woman stomping on me harder and harder while the glow of sadistic lust waxes greater and greater in her eyes, under the ruse that she is teaching me a self-defense technique, to know this. I have a reasonable capacity for logic

P.S. Here's an enlightening quote from a woman in the news. "We were just playing around." or maybe it was, "We were just having fun." Same thing at any rate. Courtesy of Lindy England of her activities at Abu Ghraib prison, Iraq.

New Generation

Editor:

From the defiant toddler melting down in the toy aisle yelling, "I want it!" to the youth demanding everything with extreme expectation of entitlement and concomitant placation, children in control are out of control.

My generation was supposed to be different, but what have we taught our children?

"Survival of the fittest," the primary secular myth, that demands relentless competitiveness, amoral winning, and a belief that what you have is what you are seems, sadly, to have remained alive and well. But Darwin's theory was misinterpreted and misused by the robber baron and colonialist culture of his time. Read <u>Darwin's Lost Theory of Love</u> by David Loye. Pushing the End Times and waiting for the Messiah is a cop-out too.

Over-reacting to the long-denied fact of child abuse, we fear to "traumatize" our children with any limits. An important book dealing with this issue is, <u>The Epidemic</u> by Robert Shaw. Complementary to this is <u>The Myth of Laziness</u> by Mel Levine.

We have substituted television, the plug-in drug, for human engagement and become addicts ourselves. If repetition is indeed the key to learning, what but the lowest-common-denominator does television now represent? (Once upon a time it was on a high enough level to commission the opera <u>Amahl and The Night Visitors</u> by Gian-Carlo Menotti. We've fallen a long way from that.) Video games represent yet more dehumanizing violence. People claim that television and video games do not create violence. If they do not, they certainly do not offer any solutions to it either. We have a whole self-help movement telling us to access the power of our subconscious minds, reprogramming ourselves with positive thinking for success and confidence with the repetition of endless pep talks and mantras. How can we believe one kind of repetition is effective and another is not?

You want eye-hand coordination? Try music and art. You have something real when you're done, maybe even your own imagination. What goals have our children learned to strive for? To be rich and famous, or humane and creative? Have we taught empathy; an ethos of facilitating each other in community to become their own best person and sharing that fullness of being creatively and joyously, or have we been defeated by the old hierarchy of winner/loser and devil take the hindmost?

We have been co-opted into another sad detour of which Enron was a major symptom. Where is the reprieve this time when it is being acted out by the highest, "Where are the WMDs" jokester in the land?

Confessions of a Luddite

June 28, 2005

Recently listened to a program on Jefferson radio, with the author, about the book <u>"Everything Bad Is Good For You."</u>

First, I'll admit to being somewhat of a Luddite even though I couldn't use a conventional typewriter flawlessly to save my life. I think things would have been better in this world if we had stopped at windmills, sailing ships (though I expect operating them must have been really a bear) trains, and water wheels. Nothing much wrong with canals instead of highways either. The U.S. did start in that direction–I saw the long-derelict canals when I visited my cousins in Ohio.

1)   The earth's natural frequencies, hence those to which we are naturally attuned in our evolution, are millions of times slower than the artificial electronic frequencies the entire planet is now bombarded with. Our bodies and our brains are electromagnetic. I believe we are healed by natural settings such as being in the forest, because we are farther there from the intensity of the fields of computers, televisions, and all manner of other junk (Navy sonar, cell towers, for instance, and navigation frequencies used for triangulation,

etc.) Childhood leukemia rates have been documented as increasing in the vicinity of radio towers. In fact, when the Vatican radio station increased its power, people around it became very alarmed and wanted to shut it down because of the increase in leukemia.   2) As we think, so we are. Some people do take this to extremes, blaming people, for instance, with catastrophic illness for "choosing" to be ill because they had some "lesson" to learn. That's garbage. If we appear able to learn or grow from being ill, it is because the human mind is so capable of salvaging lessons from difficulty, not because we "chose" to learn something in that particular way. Nonetheless, all our self-help books and much ancient teaching besides, is full of admonitions to practice positive thought, affirmations, prayer, etc. We literally create channels in our brains by our habitual thoughts. Where does water, or energy, flow but down the path of least resistance? Video games and television programs and movies full of violence are entraining our brains to think (and fear) in these terms. How many times do we have to see a 200 pound 12-year-old sitting in his darkened room, hours on end, responding with sadistic laughter over and over again to agonized screams of dying women to know this?

An environment we can control inside a box will keep us exactly there–inside a box. I can recall when I used to get stoned and watch quite a bit of T.V. (A period of about three years in my life from 17 to 19, and being the typical Treckie my first semester of college.) As I began to realize the difference between being outside in reality and fixated on the box, I felt I was literally trying to expand my horizons and get my head out of a box. I stopped using dope when I was 19 (it had been a learning experience that I fortunately outgrew) and haven't looked back. I haven't watched television since Data stabbed Counselor Troy–that was the last straw. I now am doing a lot of historical research, art, and music (among other things–including earning a living) and find myself with absolutely no time for television even if I had an interest. When I happen to be in the presence of one I usually become a) distracted and b) horrified because I literally can't be in the presence of a television for five minutes without seeing some kind of violent, lowest- common-denominator-crap that I do not want in my brain/mind. I have plenty going on inside–I don't need even half the external over-stimulation that most people in this culture crave. It drives me nuts.

The author being interviewed was obviously unfamiliar with the book <u>Evolution's End</u> by Chilton Pierce. It is a really essential book and I recommend it. Pierce also wrote <u>Four Arguments For The Elimination of Television</u>, another essential book. I did not get exposed to television until I was 8-years-old. Still too young, but not so bad as being babysat by one from the age of two. The brain constantly supplied with outside imagery does not develop the capacity (channels) to imagine and visualize or self-stimulate and will likely continue to rely on outside (manipulated) images and stimulation (advertising!) all its life.

Finally, I think a good program would be one on ADD. I'm just reading two books on the subject, <u>Healing ADD</u> by Daniel Amen, M.D. and <u>Attention Deficit Disorder</u> by Tom Hartmann. They would have a lot of disagreement with each other–especially regarding the nature of ADD (is it "illness" or is it part of our evolutionary heritage?) but both agree that large numbers of the people who wind up in our prisons are undiagnosed ADD sufferers. They would also argue over SPECT brain imaging, which Dr. Amen swears by as clearly showing the electrical activity of the brain and where it is deficient in different types of ADD, and the horror of injecting children's brains with radioactive materials in order to do such imaging; the stand Mr. Hartmann would take. I was led to the subject when a friend I work for said that cocaine and video games activate the same areas of the brain, and she loaned me Dr. Amen's book when I asked her where the statement came from. Possibly Chilton Pierce could be included in such a presentation as well–though that might well be too many at once and Chilton Pierce concentrates on the negative aspects of media in general and on children, while the others are speaking primarily about ADD and the effects of television and video games on persons with ADD.

Perilous Times

Editor:

Few doubt that we are living in peculiar and perilous times. Many long for the idyllic world of Dick and Jane, neighborhood harmony, security, intact families, the images of the 50's. Paradoxically, today we think we can grab this dream if only we are cutthroat enough in our competitiveness to be "winners", erect fences of Darwinian self-righteousness, as well as literal fences, caring little that the devil indeed takes the hindmost in the form of alcohol and drug self-medication and poverty.

The idylls of the 50's, if indeed idylls they were, with their racist and sexist oppression, were not created by the spirit of competitive, ostentatious, you-are-what-you-have, greed that now dominates our culture. Government supplemented housing and the GI Bill were available for housing and education.

On the other hand, the perfectly able-bodied, seemingly unwilling to apply any creative effort to their lives, making, "you-owe-us-food money-'scuse-me-while-I-smoke-this-cigarette" demands of passers-by, no matter how hand-to-mouth our own labors may be, is not appealing either.

As has historically been the case in other economic downturns, scapegoating of women who are employed or seeking education (witness the increase of violence in pornography in the 30's) to drive them back into the home hasn't gone away. Neither has the closed feedback loop of glamor and machismo. The habitual need for an external enemy to consolidate the control of the privileged class over labor, as we now have a war on terrorism to replace the war on communism, remains in place. One wonders how much of a witch hunt this is going to turn into as the drive for oil, and control by big oil of alternative energy sources, continues unabated.

We need to take a real look at our ecological situation. This time around, if we don't get out of our ruts and into some real solutions, the people going back to the stone-age are not going to be only the terrorists we bomb, but all of us.

Arts Under Siege

Dear Senator:

Today, artists are a community under siege. Perhaps this is not a siege which is so unique historically, after all artists have long been expected to starve in a garret. But why, in the richest nation the world has ever seen, should this be expected to be the case?

What is the measure of civilization after all? How many

bombs we can build, how many "swamps" we can pave, how many multimillionaire financiers we can bail out to the tune of billions in tax dollars, unconscionably burdening future generations with unpayable debts?

When I say we are a community under siege, I am not referring only to those who love the arts and those who create them, but to the whole of this nation. Of course some people would rather cut down forests, and beef out in front of a television set with a beer and a government subsidized cigarette, but is this what we truly want for our country and our world? I say not! Our nation has a tremendous heritage of arts, not only from Europe, but Asia, South America, Africa, and Native Americans as well. Even the smallest communities enjoy their amateur choirs, theaters, and small galleries showing local artists, and art and crafts fairs, and music festivals. All of us are continually inspired by small theater companies, such as Dell Arte in Blue Lake, for instance, and dance companies, and University groups such as Humboldt Choral that are open to the public which give many the opportunity to participate in singing the finest music who, by their dedication, keep the quality of the arts high and lively. Without these professional, if small, groups and teachers much of the general public's opportunities to grow as individuals and artists themselves will be curtailed.

Some of the senators who want to cut the arts – and this means museum exhibits, opera, dance and theater companies, and symphony orchestras-don't object to subsidizing tobacco farmers, yet they also would be the first to proclaim that they want to get tough on drugs.

Why do people use drugs? Many reasons, but I think the primary reason is because their natural joy – which comes from opportunities to develop skills, and express and grow in creative endeavors, which certainly include the arts, are never given a chance. The arts, after all, are essential to a fully realized human and humane civilization. If the government is so strapped for money, why not take the money out of tobacco subsidies and give it to the National Endowment for the Humanities? Such a step would improve both the nation's physical and mental health and save millions in health care costs as diseases such as lung cancer and emphysema would surely be greatly reduced. And how lovely it would be if young people could be encouraged to be more creative and confident rather than falling into the trap of advertisers who push smoking as glamorous and "in" as so-called "choice."

Religious Wars

Editor:

A recent letter proclaimed that Islam is involved in wars all over the world. If the U.S. is, as it claims, a Christian nation, then its covert operations in support of repressive dictatorships that have led to hundreds of thousands of deaths, and many open wars since World War II, mean that Christianity can be said to be involved in wars all over the world as well. Never mind the Crusades, the Inquisition, witch hunts, 1492, and the destruction of the Native Americans. Judaism too is a religion of peace, yet the behavior of the Israeli army and the Ultra-Orthodox, many of whom are Americans, in the occupation of the West Bank and Gaza is a disgrace, as is the occupation itself. Hinduism, the religion which gave Gandhi to the world, is engaged in tit for tat with Moslems in India.

Every religion, like every person and nation, has its bullying, self-righteous, militant side. Now, more than ever, at this impending sea change of history, each of us must choose simply either the path of kindness or cruelty.

The downtrodden are sick to death of being so, but must choose between lashing out in blind violence or principled non-cooperation. The privileged must examine their own sense of entitlement and conspicuous consumption and realize the truth about the field of blood in which they stand. Being downtrodden doesn't automatically equate to being righteous any more than being privileged does. All of us must now strive to truly engage the highest principles of whatever religion we espouse. This is not an issue of either righteousness or privilege. It is an issue of survival.

Depleted Uranium

Editor:

Depleted uranium is a waste product of the process that produces enriched uranium. It is toxic and remains radioactive with a half-life of 4.5 billion years. It is so abundant in the U.S. that it is being given away by the government to arms manufacturers. Denser than lead, shells made from DU metal easily penetrate steel. When it strikes steel it burns, spewing radioactive uranium oxide in aerosol form, particles smaller than viruses that can be inhaled or ingested for miles around.

The U.S. Army Environmental Policy Institute reported in 1995, "If DU enters the body, it has the potential to generate significant medical consequences." At least 600,000 pounds of DU and uranium dust were left around Iraq, Kuwait, and Saudi Arabia by the U.S. and British forces during the first Gulf War. DU is considered a contributing cause to the 130,000 cases of Gulf War syndrome. Of 251 Gulf War veteran's families surveyed, 67 percent of the children born to them have birth defects, some identical to those found in Iraq. European troops who served in the Balkans, where approximately 31,000 rounds of DU ammunition were used, are dying of leukemia. DU is also used to shield tanks, including the M1 Abrams tank. After 64 12-hour days, the amount of radiation a tank driver receives to his head from overhead armor will exceed the Nuclear Regulatory Commission's standard for public whole-body annual exposure to man-made sources of radiation. Clean-up after the use of these weapons is not a real option.

It should be clear from this alone that the planet can no longer afford war. Human efforts must be directed to assuaging the causes of war. We must feed, clothe, house, educate, provide health care and clean water to billions of people as well as clean up the environment. I hope enough people needed to get this real job done will be able to dedicate themselves to doing so. Alas for those fools who find this either a boring, unheroic, or unpatriotic prospect.

<u>REFERENCES</u>

<u>Metal of Dishonor</u> Eds. John Catalintto and Sara Flounders

<u>Hegemony or Survival</u> by Noam Chomsky

U.S. Decline

Dear Editor:

Many people are able to rightly point to serious destructive forces that underlie the decline of the U.S. that equally create the terrifying world conditions of which this decline is a part. Because we tend to see both in a fragmentary way, and often have a deep need for simplification in a world that can be overwhelmingly complex, we tend to focus on one thing to scapegoat.

A logger comes puffed up and bragging, "I killed 600 trees today and boy am I feeling good about it," and continues to brag about his wages. Bystanders agree, "You can't beat that," and sympathize over the condition of his hands. They were the color of wet cement. Apparently this is happening on LP land in Big Lagoon using helicopter crews from Oregon operating even at the height of a storm.

When this poor fellow is out of work because there are no trees left to kill, and all the profits are in the pockets of multimillionaires he'll never meet, undoubtedly, he won't see any connection between the policies of the multinationals like LP ripping off U.S. resources, just as they have Third World resources, while ignoring any pleas of the local populace for creation of a sustainable economy based on conservation of our resources, such as Pacific Lumber practiced before the takeover by Maxxam, rather than the boom and bust economy of over cutting, the profits of which pay off Horowitz's junk bonds. He'll blame environmentalists.

We want to know why our children are in such despair about their future that they turn to drugs. We want to know why our families are falling apart. We want to know why there is a crisis in ethics. The answers go beyond the impact of multinationals on our economy, though they do play a large part. It takes some effort to find real answers, and scapegoating the poor, women, racial minorities, and immigrants, has always afforded a quicker, easier fix.

If we want to weather this storm, this is an error we cannot continue to indulge.

Hearts of Stone

Editor:

In every religion one may find wisdom, loveliness, and generosity that strengthen our day to day resolve to relate to other living beings with patience, kindness, and to keep ourselves whole in the face of adversity. Equally, one may find all the conceits of the reptilian mid-brain, manipulating, bullying, producing history's monstrosities. These things do not reside in religions but in the heart.

W.B. Yeats wrote, "Too long a sacrifice can make a stone

of the heart." Ezekiel wrote, "I will take out of your flesh the heart of stone and give you a heart of flesh."

Many walk in bitterness that is not of their own making. There is no simple psychological rule for who among us will have a heart of flesh or a heart of stone, who will internalize the whims of popular culture or the atrocious aspects of traditional cultures, or how respond to the ignorance, narcissism or violence of one's parents.

We all want a different world from the one we have. Many of our dogmas about creating it are based sadly on projection. The more we project black hats, the more likely it is that we are carrying out the very perversions we decry in the name of ending them. History demonstrates that.

The greatest thinkers among us all refused to allow persecution to turn them into haters. This is not to be equated with nonresistance. Gandhi said, "Whatever you do may be insignificant, but it is extremely important that you do it." It is these whom we must emulate, lighting our small candles of kindness and creativity. We may never know the fruit, but light will bear its fruit as surely as cruelty and stupidity do.

Police

Editor:

How we view the members of our community who work as police officers depends on how we have experienced them, or imagined them, or both. Are they protectors of the citizenry, defenders of law and order? Fascist bullies? Corrupt or true? Surrogates for the parents we rebelled against as frustrated teenagers? Narrow-minded enforcers of the status quo? Beleaguered facilitators of a semblance of harmony in a diverse and divided society?

All of the above. Any officer can fall at various points on the scale from fascist to saint at various times, as do most of us citizens. The bottom line is fear. We live in a society that is fed a constant diet of fear, mostly by television networks like Fox, though there is no shortage of movies in the same mold. Could we all turn off the electronic drugs (video games produce the same brain wave patterns as cocaine) that fog our brains, along with alcohol and other drugs, and try to learn to communicate and listen?

Television may give young people a lot of sophisticated information, but it interferes with crucial neural development having to do with our own capacity to imagine. Without the capacity to imagine how it is to be in another person's shoes, it is pretty hard to develop empathy and compassion whether you are a police officer or a dread-locked rag bag.

Are there real bad guys out there? You bet. And thanks to the police, I don't have to deal with them. Are there paranoid people who look upon any but the narrowest variations in appearance with fear and disgust? Yep. As intelligent citizens of every stripe, we have a major endeavor in the survival of our world, and that is to grow in whatever way we can so that our fears do not reduce us all to the level of psycho barking dogs.

World of Ambiguity

Editor:

Surely no thinking person doubts that we live in a world of unbearable ambiguity, torn between beauty and horror, or that we are creatures aching for certainty and security. There are two ways people can choose to bear living in this world: escapism and sobriety. We all need a break sometimes, but habitual use of any intoxicant closes down spiritual growth and awareness. Escapism appears to have many faces, yet has but one. Sobriety may appear dull, but is multifaceted and creative. In sobriety we open ourselves to the universe, at least if we are paying attention. Drunk or stoned, we are closing ourselves down. Maybe some do need to close themselves down if their pain, either mental or physical, is that intense and they do not have other effective tools or resources to deal with it. But it has been both my experience and observation that, under the influence of drugs and/or alcohol, development of creative resources to deal with our pain—the huge, long-term processes of the pain of the human condition, isn't happening.

A little weekend cocaine is more than a "good time". It is the dissected body of a person who may have died getting the stuff here in swallowed condoms and the destruction of the fabric of entire nations. A little meth is more than a way of maintaining a competitive edge. It is pollution of the wilderness and addicted babies. Alcohol is more than a bit of relaxation. It can be fetal alcohol syndrome and babies who grow up with no impulse control. Marijuana, while it may have genuine medical usefulness, is a perpetually fogged mind and often paranoia. Tobacco sells itself as glamorous. Try looking glamorous in the middle of a bronchospasm. That is a condition of emphysema where the lungs go into seizure and you can't get air either in or out. In an experiment conducted in English prisons, persons who habitually used cocaine were given a concentrated form of nicotine. They were unable to distinguish it from cocaine. Marijuana, habitually smoked, can lead to emphysema just as tobacco does.

Some like to fantasize that what goes into one's mouth does not corrupt, only what comes out. The truth is, it is a two way street. Unless we face the fact that our deep wounding, whatever its sources on both the individual and cultural levels, is corruption that flies in the face of our birthright of pure spirit, we cannot engage the healing process. Rather, we multiply the woes of our children trying to escape our own. The real rebels in this world are sober.

History & Propaganda

Editor:

History is simplified story. Propaganda is an even more simplified story. In structuring our realities we generally choose to believe the simpler stories, the ones that allow us to feel heroic about ourselves. Unfortunately, that tends to prevent correcting a wrong path and thus creating a more genuine basis for how we value ourselves as individuals, nations, and cultures. Ultimately, internalized culture shapes our realities and the values we seek to emulate.

The dark side of American culture is about winning, i.e. hierarchy, expressed through the closed feedback loop of bullying-machismo and back-stabbing glamour. This is increasingly hard to alter as so many people are literally hypnotized by their television sets and the media are increasingly owned by fewer and fewer strictly commercial interests exploiting, indeed creating, the desire to live up to these images. Thus many live in crass oblivion to the needs of the life around them, too full of every kind of speed to treasure the boredom of sustaining and maintaining.

Nonetheless, people against war in Iraq, and the last 50

years of CIA blowback wars, question this media-hyped reality. Is Saddam a good guy? No, but he was funded by the CIA, as was the Taliban. Does being against war mean support for Saddam? Hardly.

What will save this world? Education, health care, investment in a restoration economy and housing; or bombs, prisons and the imposition of the black and white thinking of fundamentalism? It is time we learned to live with the openness, honesty, and integrity and dedication to democracy that we proclaim, and to pursue peace and justice. Otherwise, Mother Earth will indeed be shaking out her sad skirts.

Spew Forth

Editor:

Given the incessant spewing of inanities our president treats us to, one tends to become a little numb, but was anyone paying attention when he declared open season on people over 55? "You folks under 55 are going to lose out (quoting loosely here) because of old guys like me." Smirk, smirk. Well, George, we all know you are going to be protected by the Secret Service the rest of your life, but the rest of us over 55's aren't so privileged. While I believe we may have managed to raise a generation even more obsessed with privilege, entitlement, and materialistic measures of the survival of the presumed fittest than we were, admittedly these attitudes are not really new. I know this because long ago in my idealistic youth I asked another young woman,

"If everyone had their needs met for housing, food, clothing, etc. would you steal?" Her answer was yes, because having more would make her better than me. Most of us, hopefully, know this is a false premise, except of course the people who are presently running the country.

I believe the attack by Bush on Social Security has a two-fold purpose. The primary is, of course, to put the money that our generation has struggled to pay into the system, which is now becoming due back to us from a trust fund that will still be able to pay out 75 percent of benefits by 2045 just as it is, into the pockets of his buds on Wall Street. The other, call me paranoid if you will, is to get rid of people who, being over 55, were not entirely robotized by television, video games, and militaristic brain washing, into believing killing is fun.

American culture divides our world between so called winners and losers. The "winners" are full of fear because they must exhaust themselves on the treadmill of possessing more and more in order to remain "superior," while they develop few, if any, inner spiritual creative resources to feed their true hunger. There are many reasons one becomes a "loser" in this "game." Overweening belief in entitlement and concomitant failure to develop viable productivity accounts for some. Others are so beaten down when aging and best effort still leaves them discounted, after a life time of being discounted, bullied and stabbed in the back by the winners, either because they internalize this belief system (and so turn to drugs and alcohol) or exhaustion. Thus the "winners" eliminate much of their competition, not by their own successful efforts to excel, but by stopping others from having a role, to the detriment of a genuinely creative, humane culture. Now we are all like sheep being led to slaughter, not the abundant life which is the birth right of all. Ultimately it all plays into the hands of the ruling elite, as it always has.

Reflecting on Trump

Editor:

Whole nations are on the brink of famine because of American-backed bombing campaigns and arms sales (Yemen and South Sudan), yet many of us continue to think of ourselves in idyllic terms of Norman Rockwellian visions of innocence. We are bidden to give up our privacy for the sake of safety and expected to crow along with Trump over the blood money we will receive from multibillion dollar arms sales to Saudi Arabia, our so-called ally who is, in fact, the source of Whhabism—militant Islam—spreading through the world and from where eleven of the 9/11 hijackers actually came.

This nation is founded on wonderful ideals—though it always excluded women, blacks, and Native peoples. It is also founded on slaughter and slavery. Now the proposed Republican "health" plan will give huge tax breaks to the richest 400 families while cutting elders, children, and disabled. It is not a health plan but a tax break for the rich, crafted behind closed doors.

I recall some of what my education was in grade and high school. We were told that Native people made clay pots and lived in teepees. We made some clay pots in imitation. That was 3rd grade. That was it. World War II got three pages in the high school social studies book. I doubt we'd even get that much from privatized education.

Now with the recension of DACA, 800,000 young people are to be denied the education that would enable them to be fully contributing members of our country. For many this is the only country they have known because they were driven from their own countries by gang violence fueled by U.S. craving for drugs—cocaine that gives the edge in super competition for the hideous dominance culture we have come to substitute for God.

The only thing Trump voters are to be congratulated for is reviving the Civil War that was fought to preserve a slave-holding South that hoped to create an empire of its own and the election of an American Hitler.

I am old enough to remember the difference between the way the sun feels on my skin now, and the way it felt when I could lay out on my porch in the summer sun for longer than five minutes. I am dumfounded at our current situation, but I have finally come to a conclusion. There may be little hope even now, but if we do not take congress back in 2018 from these purveyors of ignorance, arrogance, greed, and racism, it is over for both America and the planet. Well, maybe the planet can be expected to recover in a few million years, but we won't be here to see it.

Internalized Patriarchy

January 23, 2017

Kathy Lopez's quotation of Miami Catholic doctor Grazie Christie denigrating modern feminism as "superficial and banal" on the basis of a Saturday Night Live satire, is a "full display" of the mentality of women who have internalized patriarchal attitudes toward their own gender. I have never watched Saturday Night Live, so I cannot comment on the skit she is claiming as proof of their contention. There is no doubt that earlier feminists had a long row to hoe, but if anybody seriously thinks the job is done or that modern feminists do not passionately engage major issues, take a look at who just got elected president. Many women came forward to tell how he had molested them, yet women voted for him. Why? One said it would mean she was attractive if someone grabbed her private parts. That is internalized patriarchy. Such an act is not an expression of desire or attraction, it is an act of aggression intent on dominance.

Regarding the issue of abortion, unfortunately women sometimes become pregnant against their will; sometimes in good faith with a partner who abandons them, sometimes with a partner who is abusive mentally, physically, or economically (or all three) or who does not himself want the child, which can increase the abuse in a relationship. To force a woman to bear a child she cannot care for or who, for any reason, simply is not ready to be a mother, is the wrong choice for any society. The vocation of woman? Being a mother is certainly an honorable and, hopefully, in as reasonable a measure as is humanly possible, a joyful one. But is being a father the vocation of man? Human beings, regardless of gender, have many vocations. Reproduction is only one of them.

"Peace begins in the womb," she says. I think that's a

good statement. So what peace can come for an unwanted child facing poverty, abuse, violence and patriarchal denigration of his or her mother as a "slut" or "whore?" That remains the attitude toward a woman who has had "too many" boyfriends, let along one who winds up pregnant. And yet, they keep trying to take away birth control too.

There are seven billion of us on the planet. We have passed the carrying capacity of our world, especially if everyone wants a middle class American lifestyle. Let the children be born who are desired and who have a reasonable chance of being adequately cared for. If a woman is poor and alone, and still wants her child, by whatever means her pregnancy came to her, then she must find her way and hopefully there is support in place for such children and they will not be denigrated as "sniveling welfare bums and cheats." But there can be no romantic idealization of such circumstances as "woman's vocation" no matter how many "adorable" baby showers she is given. Being a parent is not a vocation, it is a calling and hopefully more than a biological one.

In a country dedicated to endless war, as we have now come to be, which considers fifty percent of its budget, billions of dollars, going to the military as "neglect" of our armed forces, I think that the demand that women bear every pregnancy to full term, even if it may kill them, is not a celebration of life but a demand for an economic draft and an endless supply of cannon fodder.

ESSAYS

Mutual Needs

What men and women mutually need in relationships is tenderness, kindness, honesty, open communication, supportiveness, respect, and good will. When we fail to achieve these qualities, we blame various social and religious causes. The Right decries "loss of values" and tries to cram everyone back into the Victorian straight jacket. The Left proclaims free love and tries to guilt-trip women into bed as "up-tights" if they resist.

The Right bombs women's clinics, tries to eliminate birth control, and tells us our natural sexuality is evil. The Left proclaims we are "sexual beings" and considers anyone who is not sexually active to be warped, thus shaming women into unwanted sex. "If you refuse me, honey you'll lose me. Then you'll be all alone," isn't exactly a new line either.

I have never defined myself as a sexual being. If I choose not to express sexuality I don't feel diminished as a human being. That I cannot express it, even when I have been invited to, without being smirked at, hated, or called "slut" and dumped, does make me feel diminished.

Men worry so much about how to be men and the stock cultural answer has been hierarchic machismo. The nurturing and compassion that we all often lack, has rightfully been proclaimed to no longer be a singularly female virtue or prerogative. Relationships largely remain stuck in the traditional sadomasochistic addictive roles of our culture. Both men and women separate their sexuality from their affections in order to be in control and end up treating each other as objects. Women still treat each other as rivals rather than comrades.

If we truly relate, companionship is the exchange for companionship. The only service we owe each other is a compassionate and vigilant honesty that facilitates our owning our processes, perceptions, and projections. Children should be brought in, not to serve our old age, as one woman proclaimed, but to be the best they can be for humanity and themselves.

If we fall into a backlash of oppression, as clinic bombings and doctor murders proclaim that we are, everybody loses. I'd still like to see a world where children can look at the roses and the sky and really be free, free to be joyous, sensuous (realize that sensuality and sexuality are not always the same thing) and creative; to grow up nurtured and nurturing regardless of their gender.

SOME REFLECTIONS FROM TORAH STUDY

How should we understand the various sacred texts of the world? Many interpret the scriptures literally. It says plainly what it says, it is what it is. There are also long traditions both in the East and the West that scriptures contain hidden, symbolic meanings that the sincere student must dig for as for gold or jewels.

Were the scriptures written by men (priests/scribes) for their own times and purposes, or were they divinely inspired for all time and are these categories necessarily exclusive of each other? If there is deep spiritual symbolism in scriptures, was it purposely put there by the authors or was it read in later by people struggling to make the writings meaningful for their own times? Perhaps such a struggle in itself led to an unfolding of mind and/or mind-set that served the evolutionary/Divine purpose. The very concept of the existence of a Divine will, plan, or purpose or, for those who prefer to think in terms of higher evolution, interpreted as it is usually from an anthropomorphic point of view, can in itself be questioned. That is not my present purpose, however.

I am qualified to address two sorts of things: My personal experience and what I can logically extrapolate from my studies. Regarding the ultimate "plan" of the universe, be it seen as manifesting Diving Mind or billions of years of evolutionary accidents, I have beliefs about aspects of it. However, I do not care to make dogmatic pronouncements about it. Whatever the plan of the universe, we must simply do our best to live the best life we can here and now. Ethically, for instance, after I die it is of no consequence whether I will simply cease to exist, may go to heaven or hell, live on some other plane of reality, or will be reincarnated in some form. I am obliged as an ethical being, as a conscious being, to live the most positive life I can. I cannot be overly concerned with what is beyond my power. True morality derives from love of life/God, not fear of hell.

I think it is probable that, whatever their source or purpose, the original writers of scriptures wrote them to be read literally. For example, the Temple Scroll, one of the Dead Sea Scrolls, describes a Temple, the building of which would have required the filling in of the Kedron Valley east of Jerusalem and a lot of excavation on the west, removing tons of rock by means of human labor. Taken beside such ancient works as the pyramids of Egypt and the Great Wall of China, this temple, which would have dwarfed Solomon's, they probably were literally serious. We are, however, looking at a long process. There are very old traditions of symbolic interpretation as well and a tradition that the originally oral stories had attached symbolic interpretations that only the initiate knew, and these occult (meaning simply "hidden") oral traditions have been largely lost over the centuries. Certainly this is true of the New Testament's writings as gentile Christians did not receive the Jewish oral traditions that explain them, and they were largely lost as Jewish Christians were reabsorbed into the main body of Judaism.

Certainly people who interpret scripture literally have deep religious experience and faith just as does the mystic. As a student of history though, I do not believe any ancient writing can be understood outside of its historical context. Just as in our own time there are political, economic, population/migration pressures; myriad belief systems, both religious and secular, and military institutions, which all constitute factors influencing what people believe and experience, and how they act in any given era or situation. So too in ancient times. We cannot even interpret Mother Goose, which is only a few hundred years old and of a relatively familiar culture, without some understanding of the history of the time in which the rhymes were written. How much less so a totally foreign culture and language that is 3000 years old? In granting respect to any interpretation of scripture, we must then ask what is the bottom line. My answer is this: Would you be willing to kill somebody over this?

As I see it, the problem with most fundamentalism,

and literal interpretation of such things as the return of Christ, the rebuilding of the Temple and/or the reinstitution of animal sacrifice there, or the End of Days and the coming of the Messiah with the hosts of heaven (the break-through into our world by the hosts of heaven, who would fight beside the ritually pure remnant of Israel to rid the Holy Land of the Romans, was the literal expectation of the Essenes of Qumran and the Jesus movement); the legendary battle between the gods of good and evil (Satan and Jehovah) both in Heaven and on Earth, or that the Jews rejected/killed Christ, etc. is that a large number of the holders of these beliefs, as literal, are willing to kill and/or condemn to hell those who don't agree with them. Most people of less literal persuasion generally are not.   The fundamentalists should not be surprised that the kind of harm their belief system causes provokes hostility.   Dogmatic literal beliefs have been the cause of mass murder, torture, and religious persecution and wars throughout history.

For the sake of discussion I will set aside these facts of history. If that is what one's experience and learning lead one honestly to, and the potential for killing and persecution because of such beliefs is indeed set aside (that is, their fulfillment is left to God) then they are as right as any other. I would rather seek to examine instead the idea of symbolic versus literal interpretation of sacred writing and ritual practices from the point of view of intrinsic value (i.e. to what behaviors do these beliefs extrapolate) to the degree I am able.

We live our lives on the models of our parents, on the basis of faith, inner experience, or what our studies and life experiences have brought us to understand, or the combination thereof. I cannot despise the atheist because he/she has not had a mystic experience of the presence of God. For whatever reason, they may or may never have such an experience or be able to understand my mystic view any more than I can understand how they can look at the world and not see God. I do not believe that the Creator demands of anyone to believe in something they haven't experienced or understood, since I don't believe that the Creator demands anything of us not in line with ethical integrity. It is moral character which is the bottom line in either case. It may be argued that a percentage of humanity is kept from wickedness only by fear of punishment (whether jail or hell) and they must be thus forced to conform to the expectations of society whether they understand or care about moral integrity or not. This is sadly true, but quite apart from the imposition of a dogma or belief system that is not freely arrived at.

Idolatry is a major issue in Western scripture, so I'd

like to start by taking a look at that. Idolatry can be understood in a number of ways. We keep all kinds of objects around us. American homes are such a veritable clutter that Japanese have wondered why we like to have our homes as if they were museums. Objects impart or implement an exchange of energy, or activation of mental processes such as memory of a beloved aunt's last visit. Is it any less "idolatrous" to have on one's wall the picture of Jesus symbolically knocking for entry to the "door" of our hearts that gives the Christian comfort in salvation and exemplifies the belief that all one has to do for salvation is to invite their Lord into their heart, that indeed this is the only path to salvation; and a home alter with a statue of the Buddha surrounded by flowers, candle, and incense that reminds the Buddhist of the compassion of the Buddha who forsook Nirvana to remain in the world as a teacher, and the Bodhisattva potential in all, which inspires compassion for all living creatures to be led into Nirvana, escaping from the rounds of rebirth and suffering? Though the religious concepts behind these images differ, they also clearly have a commonality of compassion.

According to Julian Jaynes in <u>The Origin of Consciousness In The Breakdown of The Bicameral Mind</u>, the idolatry that figures so large in the Bible as an abomination came about because of changes in social structure brought about by contacts between peoples whose societies were very different. Thus they could no longer rely on the voices of their gods for guidance and structure. He postulates that they literally heard these "godly" voices through the speech center (which is not symmetrical in the human brain since the right and left sides function differently) in the right side of the brain, and from which the voices of the schizophrenic even today emerge. As society grew more complex, people could no longer rely on the unconscious parental voice of their god, and so built idols to try and trigger the voices that once had guided them but no longer could in the face of new complexities. They slowly had to develop consciousness to guide their lives instead. This is a very interesting idea whether one believes it or not. I see the real problem being one in which we give our power over to the authority of another so that our consciousness (always rather weak at best) and sense of responsibility for our actions and the consequences of our actions, become even more weak.

The power we give away now is often to a lover. It can also be to that new talking idol, the television, whose advertisers tell us how we should look, behave, spend our money, etc. But that's another issue. If Jaynes is correct, the conflict then would have been between emerging consciousness and those who desperately tried to hang onto the "voices" of the old gods. If we apply it to today's world, the commandment, "You shall have no other gods before me" is directly linked to, "You shall not kill (or murder, depending on your translation) because the omnipresent God who supplanted the ancient idols, is seen as the life force and life itself is sacred, whether we see it as so because it is life or because it is suffused with God.

When we make an object, such as the rock that is said to be the one on which Abraham was prepared to sacrifice Isaac, also said to be in housed in the Dome of the Rock in Jerusalem, and which is also said to be the rock from which Mohammed lifted off in his dream (astral) journey to receive his revelations, into something we are willing to kill for, we are practicing idolatry, as we also do when we call a man God. Thus we condense God out of the universe. It was the aim of the concept of the invisibility of God, which led to the struggle against idol making, to raise our consciousness toward a capacity to realize universality of Divine presence.

The monotheistic religions all have God the Creator as the central figure of the universe. For some this Being is separate from creation like an artist from a painting or sculpture. For others of a more mystic bent, God is imminent in creation. "Where shall we turn and not see God?" is the rhetorical question which acknowledges this. Either way, the oneness of God is tantamount. The oneness of life is borne out by genetic science as the DNA molecule has proven to be the common blueprint of every form of life there is. The importance and reality of a monotheism that honors the universality of the Creator of all living and the mystic unity with the Loving Presence that supplants "my god vs your god", "my idol vs your idol" (or possession thereof) has yet to be fully implemented in our consciousness. The invisible, omnipresent Energy/Life Force/Source/Loving Divine Presence/Creative Mind of the universe concept of God, if it has an ultimate purpose, must be to move us beyond the idolatry that leads to killing, and into recognition of its universality as a reality to which the function of synagogue, church, mosque and sweat lodge all attest. If the Divine is universally present, then there can be no attachment to either object or place for the seat of the Divine. Indeed with this, raised consciousness becomes the heart or soul and its manifestation on the human plane is compassion, creativity and ethical integrity.

This is not to say that there are not power spots on the earth which facilitate prayer, such as Jerusalem, (though the origins of Jerusalem are as much political and military as spiritual). This is why Cathedrals were built on them and they should be held as sacred gifts. It may be harder to achieve the prayer state in a home, church, synagogue, or mosque that is not built in such a place. Go then and take a walk in the woods or by the sea, for Nature is strong in this regard and the act of walking itself, in such a setting, can awaken a deep response of gratitude, (great attitude) which is the realization of the unity of Divine and human blessing. This is a deep part of our essential humanity.

Prayer, whatever form it takes, requires practice and development that flows from practice; a capacity for recognition of the processes of growth and healing that are occurring within us through the practice. One may think of prayer as a tuning of the instrument which is the soul.

Different religions call different cities holy and make them places of pilgrimage. While such pilgrimages may serve as rituals which can heighten our spirituality, I believe that the vision of the holy city, the sacred landscape has more value as a symbol of the sacred and unassailable dwelling of the soul, a mandala of the completeness and creative complexity of the soul than as a physical, earthly place. Then it does not matter whether we are talking about Jerusalem, Mecca or Camelot. We really are talking about a symbol of human spiritual potential.

Some wish not only to rebuild the physical Temple but

to reinstitute animal sacrifice there as well because they see this as the literal command of God. Animal sacrifice, in its day, was a great advance over the universal practice of human sacrifice that Jews put an end to a thousand years before the surrounding cultures did. While the more primitive Israelites were busily absorbing Canaanite culture, their leaders were at great pains to keep them from taking up surrounding religious practices as well, human sacrifice being the most abhorrent. As an aside, it is from this attempt to keep religious practice separate that we get the practice of Kosher. "You shall not stew a kid in its mother's milk," originally had nothing to do with not mixing milk and meat in a single meal. (As a child who was given plenty of creamed hamburger and creamed chipped beef over mashed potatoes, I know there are no gastronomical problems with this). It had to do with not following other religions' sacrificial practices.

Life is sacred and not to be taken without dire need. For as long as people have eaten meat, others have chosen not to. Today we have plenty of people living healthy active lives (12 million in the U.S.) without consumption of flesh foods. Health and ethical ecological arguments regarding being on the top of an artificial food chain that feeds tons of grain to cattle while millions of people are malnourished aside, to believe that God desires animal sacrifice must be among the most base of superstitions, especially in our own time when such devices are no longer needed to wean people away from human sacrifice. Human sacrifice was always a power trip by black magicians and the priests of certain religions and remains so. Its modern equivalent is telling people they will be sent to Hell by God (essentially making of God a Sadist) for not believing in such and such a dogma. In the dramatic rituals that surrounded it I'm sure it triggered intense endorphin flow as well, which can be mistaken for "religious" experience. Pornography, orgies, sacrifice (animal or otherwise) self-mutilation, torture all orchestrate the dark side of our being, may stimulate bliss and oblivion but, like any good drunk, have to be repeated and do not develop the ethical dimension of true spirituality, or genuine happiness, only intensity.

Both in the negative and the positive, it can thus be seen that ritual is a two way path. It has been argued rightly that ritual can activate consciousness and genuine experience. I experience from the practice of Japanese Tea Ceremony for example, calming, centering, timelessness which results from concentration on a series of memorized movements; meaningless until the experience it shapes is manifest. So also with the keeping of the Sabbath, a day in which we relax, become receptive instead of active, yin rather than yang, prayerful and meditative rather than caught up in the thousand and one tasks of daily living. This is something that can work beyond our understanding in the shaping and deepening of the soul but, like prayer or Tea, takes practice. What we learn in the Sabbath Palace of Stillness suffuses our life and gives us foundation in times of crisis. It is through conscious development, that the journey away from idolatry was intended to take us on, that we are guided into higher/deeper spirituality and through which we can grow to choose ethical, beneficial rituals over outmoded and destructive ones. The aim of the beneficent ritual is to shape the soul, the emotional body, as an ever deepening vessel of the Divine that is manifest as compassion, understanding, and courage. In ritual, negative or positive, we instill habits, establish channels; sequences of firing of neurons in our brains. With consciousness we can choose spiritual rather than visceral rituals. We can work to integrate the spiritual and visceral, doing the transforming work of spiritual and physical integration; that is lifting up the physical plane from mindless selfish gratification to an ethical (i.e. having a capacity to consider the global effect of actions, and the will that our actions should produce as universal of a good as possible) and finer joy that is not contaminated by the limitations of being either out of harmony with Nature (the perpetuation of life) or the hierarchical power seeking, cruelty, and destructiveness that makes that life miserable.

ETHICS AND THE PARANORMAL

We exist within a wider range of reality than we usually acknowledge in our day to day life. The reasons for this lack of acknowledgment are primarily cultural and historical. The interface of multiple realities, depth of experience, and communication regarding them, has bearing on ethical outlook. It is the ethical interface between multiple realities I presently wish to explore. I am hereby seeking to establish an objective basis for ethics that takes these realities into account.

Attempting to establish an "objective" basis for ethics is a very old human endeavor, but always something we must seek to struggle with. It is the major aspect of our "God wrestling." Ultimately, ethics are a matter of survival, for without an ethical framework by which our endeavors can be weighed, we are bound to create chaos, a waste of energy the world can less and less afford. We will create chaos anyway, but an ethics based on as wide an understanding as possible remains an essential, ongoing human effort, without which our humanity is surely diminished.

As difficult as an objective basis for ethics is, agreement on the nature of ultimate reality poses equal difficulty. Is ultimate reality the basis of ethics? Yes and no. To the degree that ultimate reality (let us say God) is unknowable, it is not, since the unknowable cannot be a referent in the development of structure, though the fact that it is unknowable can be. To the degree that we experience Divine Presence, the Holy One's Immanence as the ground of our being, our joy, our hope, it is.

If we lack the latter experience, our ethics must be based on practical human logic. Either way, whether we operate out of logic or ecstatic intensity, there is potential for breakdown. The intensity achieved through rituals of power, such as human sacrifice and war, does not produce objective ethics. Neither does the logic of materialism and hierarchy, however well they may seem to function as an operating system for society. Too much is left out and balance is never quite achieved. There is waste and loss in the system. At this point, we begin to need some definitions.

I would like to define the ethical as the most efficient and holistic use of life energy. Indeed, it cannot be efficient if it is not holistic. A primary aspect of this is, of course, the acknowledgment of the shadow within. This has been discussed at considerable length by others, but acknowledgment of it remains essential to achieve a full realization of what we are dealing with when we struggle with ethical purpose.

It is generally well known that denial of the shadow takes considerable energy and leads, through the structures of self-delusion and projection, to huge failures of ethics. The self-knowledge essential to healing these kinds of failures is a lifetime labor of vigilance and, as whole communities can become corrupt, community is not a fail-safe structure through which to achieve this. Being in a loving and intelligent community should, nonetheless, bring about a higher degree of sustainable ethical success and emotional fulfillment essential to our humanity than being without such a community as we both challenge and nurture ourselves, and each other, through community. Whatever communities we perceive ourselves to be a part of, ethics are about the ways we structure relationship.

The mind has its range of capacity and operates with the tools it receives through genetic and cultural heritage. The cultural includes the historical. Levels of intelligence, growth, potential creativity are manifest best in a brain that has grown in a well-nourished, drug-free environment so that its structures can optimally develop. There probably is a wide range of perfectly functional neural setups which cause considerable variation in how individuals perceive the world. This would be the basis of the wide range of sensitivity humans display (as do all mammals, according to Elaine Aaron, in <u>The Highly Sensitive Person</u>,) from what is labeled "psychic" to "sensitive" to "average/normal." Llyal Watson (<u>Dark Nature</u>, and <u>Supernature</u>) and Michael Murphy (<u>The Future of The Body</u>) are other authors who present the "psychic" functions as essentially biological and universal. We are also familiar with Einstein's continuum of energy and matter and the findings of quantum physics. Some would thus materialize the spiritual, and others would spiritualize the material. As is experiential for the mystic, the Holy One is the ground of our being. There is none other. Substance and energy are one. Being utterly penetrated by the Great Horror and the Ecstatic Glory is the mystic's Land of Paradox, where we fully experience these as knit together, unbearably. At this cusp is the choice and our daily life is the refinement of it. The way is narrow. Here it is possible to illustrate with a famous story: Shema Israel. There are four rivers in Paradise. Ha Shem Elohenu. Four Rabbis entered a garden together to study Kabala. One died. One went mad. One chose to follow the Dark Side. Only one emerged enlightened. Ha Shem echad. The daily life that bears the paradox and chooses to manifest the light side while understanding the roots of darkness, that is enlightenment. Enlightenment, like God, is a verb, a dynamic.

We live presently in a culture that still manifests the spirit of Rome with its bread and circuses (or perhaps in modern terms, the mall and sadomasochistic pornography) that undoubtedly finds cavorting, pastel duckies and bunnies under glitter-dusted rainbows hopelessly maudlin. Nonetheless, I confess a decided preference for the latter (found on a birthday card my aunt sent to me.) Such things can, in fact, quite delight me. So do wide open tulips, wine-scented roses, moldering leaves in the winter garden, the iridescence of sea slugs, alliterative poetry, galloping horses, mountains, the Pacific in storm, winter trees stark against the sky, spring, sleeping in the sun, children laughing in delight and discovery, and my cat, among other things. In a world of ugliness, cruelty, and horror, the ethical choice is to strive manifest beauty, kindness, and wisdom in thought (visualization) and deed, (creative and honorable labor) and relationship (family, community, world, nature.) All this may be considered "maudlin." It has little to do with the "realities" of power and hierarchy that appear to own our world. Habits of thought ultimately can make us free. They also may give the powers that be the handles they desire on our psyches.

We have many tools for changing our habits. Prayer, meditation, study, and the arts are primary among them. Can we shut down old, destructive channels, quite literally carved into our brains by electrical nerve impulses–like water carves canyons and gullies in earth? We can recognize them for what they are and refuse to allow them to manifest even while we acknowledge them and labor to outgrow what may have been programed into us as children. Indeed, they will inevitably manifest if we remain unconscious of them. That is the nature of the shadow. Acknowledging them for what they are is the basic first step out of denial and self-delusion.

Here we may be caught by the "need to experience all things,"of the hedonist claiming that all else is repression of true freedom, versus the ethical choice not to experience or manifest corruption. Here, I will need to attempt to define corruption. I suppose we are all corrupt to the degree that we have lost our innocence, but we counter this in ourselves, and our societies, to the degree that we are able to consciously choose, on the basis of responsible and honest self-knowledge, kindness over cruelty, delight over cynicism, power to rather than power over, expansiveness over bitterness, and generosity over greed. These tools (prayer, meditation, study, the arts, and nurturing relationships) need to be given to us in our childhood whenever possible, but they are not likely to be found in dysfunctional families. The emotional body is rarely reached by logic (though it remains my hope that logic may be a useful and concomitant first step to the degree that one is capable of exercising it) as anyone raising a teenager, falling in love with someone else's spouse, giving away our power in order to gain approval, or living next door to a dementor, sooner or later, becomes well aware.

We do not need to give up intensity (transcendence of the self), but we do need to be aware that we are ethically responsible for the means by which we achieve it. The world is full of corrupt and easy paths to intensity and always has been. Some of them have even been mistaken for religious experience. The paths of ethical intensity require self-discipline and patience, not the instant gratification of television-time and the habit of the lowest common denominator, namely violence. The coupling of violence with sexuality, that is, the glamorizing of acts of hatred, both toward the self, due to guilt over one's sexuality, and one's partner, maintained by the delusion that the intensity of hate is love, and pain is desired by the object, which is used as the excuse to express hatred without the burden of guilt this would normally impose, is one example of the corruption that is the underbelly of our culture. Pornography and sadomasochism are to be accounted corrupt because they express, and serve to maintain, hierarchy, self-delusion, and habitual destructiveness as a path to intensity. Here, "question your perversion" becomes as good a motto as "question reality." That is the individualized level. War is the globalized level.

What is it to glamorize? Simply to create, pretend, buy into, an illusory and self-deluding perception, possibly with great sophistication and even artistic skill, that something is what it is not. War is not peace. Flogging is not an act of love.

Logic exists on many levels. The logic we can hope to achieve as a species consists of finally integrating the intuitive and holistic ways of knowing with linear and logical ways of knowing. Both are valid but limited. I agree with others who have said this will be the next stage of our evolution. The negative side of one is superstition; the disastrous projection of hallucinated metaphor from the unconscious emotional body into the world, as I believe happened when Israel, in massive despair in the face of so many crucifixions and slaughters by Rome, literally believed that the Heavenly Host would be fighting beside them as they rebelled against Rome as long as they maintained ritual purity. The negative side of the other is dogma, both in science and religion, the equally disastrous refusal to perceive the facts of reality when they do not support one's theories. By this integration, we can expect to live with far greater intensity, carry more current if you will, joyousness and, hopefully, more genuine wisdom.

We live in a world that is far more magical than we realize. This can be terrifying, but it is a reality we need to integrate rather than deny or become either superstitious or dogmatic about. A major reason for the need to integrate these aspects of reality is to outgrow, as much as possible, the confusion and crazy-making that arises from denying them. Another reason is because we need to get out of the habit of denying reality because we cannot understand it or find it frightening. Denial of fantastic (or what would historically be called magical) reality is another form of corruption. Only living with paradox strengthens wisdom, just as striving to understand strengthens knowledge. It is to be hoped that with the growth of wisdom, we can find our way into more paths of action that are healing rather than destructive. Perhaps that is at least one reason why paradox exists.

To the best of my knowledge, a fairly high percentage of human beings have direct experience of what is termed the paranormal. These are realities we often deny either out of fear of ridicule; the belief that it means we are crazy; fear of the event itself, or the supposed implications of the event; or inability to integrate a given experience into our belief systems, (cognitive dissonance.)

For some, "paranormal" represents a descent into a terrifyingly chaotic universe. Grant that we are microbes existing on a grain of sand, whirling at the edge of a galaxy of billions of stars in a universe of billions of galaxies, about which we have an undoubtedly minuscule amount of knowledge, what have we got to lose by acknowledging another aspect of reality? It depends on how you handle it, as with everything else. To acknowledge that, in the face of mystery, and supposed chaos, we live in a self-referred system of ethical responsibility, that is to say a logical one, ethical capacity must be seen as potentially being expanded rather than negated by the fact of paradox and paranormal realities. Though at another level that is granting a lot, the aim remains self-knowledge without which there can only be limited ethical capacity.

"Paranormal" reality is not something to be denied, as science often has, or labeled as evil, as religion often has, or worshiped, as superstition often has, though there may be plenty of reason to respond in any of these ways to given individual events. A lot depends on the stories we tell ourselves about them. If we can practice tolerance in the face of paranormal paradox, how much more may we be able to practice in the face of social and cultural paradox.

I would like to use UFOs as an example since this is a fairly widespread phenomenon, something about which we have a multitude of stories, and about which I have personal experience. Since this presumed paranormal experience is a reality for me, I have done considerable research because I hoped to understand it. Thus I think I know most of the stories about them. Some people believe they are mentioned in the Bible and have always been with us. Some people believe they are extraterrestrial machines. Some believe they are psychic phenomena, others that they are multidimensional travel devices of some advanced race or races of beings that are evil (enter Darth Vader, Satan, etc.) or good (enter angels, cosmic elder brothers), that they portend Armageddon or the return of Christ. Jung believed they were subconscious projections of our desire for wholeness and thus were a form of mandala. Some believe them to be a kind of animal that lives in our stratosphere, others that they come from a hollow earth, inside of which are other continents, oceans and a central sun. My own experience validates none of these. Neither does it particularly exclude them. I doubt the earth is hollow but it may well have yet some secret places. I definitely don't accept the idea they are signs of the return of Christ. I am too much a historian for that. I have my own story about them, about which I would not be dogmatic either, though I consider it to be based on logic and some alternative reading of history, it remains science fiction–a rather paranoid science fiction at that, and the world at large has had quite enough of fantasies that resemble reality enough to lead the gullible astray without my adding to it.

I do not know why, who, what, or how they are, but I must accept their existence and realize I live in a mysterious universe which is far more powerful than I am. But all of us already know that anyway. Being open to paradox and mystery as reality is an inherent lesson in being open to the universe, whatever else it may be, which is ultimately the only basis we have for the courage to live and live more fully.

I could as well go on at some length regarding any number of other personal experiences of the paranormal. I believe they are fairly common if only we are willing to admit that they do happen. The craziness comes in, not with the fact of the experience, but with denial or the superstitions and/or dogmatic interpretations of such experiences.

Do we want to say ghosts are, in accordance with traditional interpretation, earthbound dead? I have no particular reason not to, but I don't know. I do know that both the living, and what are interpreted to be the disembodied, can interface with our nervous systems with varying degrees of intensity, but that may be ultimately biological. My mother once hit me with such a fit of rage that I was doubled over in agony though she was ten feet away and never touched me. I got it in the gut (literally) for naively passing my father's words on to her.

People cast spells on each other all the time, only now it is called bullying, charm, seduction, energy cording, psychic attack, among other things, and can be a major factor in deep communication, both positive and negative, and is not always easy to sort out from one's own projections. It is when your mind suddenly is flooded with images of a long forgotten battle, even while paying attention to some other pleasurable, singular, and positive activity (in my case listening to music on a pair of headphones in the library) and you finally are drawn to turn around to find a complete stranger staring fixedly at the back of your head, her eyes full of hate. Or you suddenly sense someone near-by wants to hit you and you turn around to discover a former friend, who now hates you because you denied her something she considered her due, in the post office line two people behind you. (I mistook this energy at first as coming from the person immediately in front of me and so stepped back thinking he may have felt I was too close to him.) It can certainly save your life when something tells you not to take your right-of-way as a pedestrian in front of a car, well before you see the driver's hate-filled face and the "America, love it or leave it" bumper sticker as she passes, anti-Viet

Nam war hippie that I was, and straight that she was. It is when you turn around for no apparent reason to find the dog staring at you through the window, silently willing to be let in, which pretty clearly demonstrates the biological basis of such experiences.

Negative spell casting takes its toll though, since to do this the person has to run those emotions through their own heart. The more time is spent controlling, manipulating and punishing others to get what they want, whatever plane it takes place on, the less time and energy they are putting into their own creative development. In short, getting a life. It remains that we must deal with the psychic through the psychic and the physical through the physical. Otherwise we wind up with witch hunts.

Are we to say near-death experiences, or presumed astral projection, are indeed our first steps back into the astral plane, either to free ourselves or to be returned to the cycle of rebirth; or rather the experience of phenomena that exist only within the still-living brain? I don't know and it has to be okay not to know. With the acceptance of not knowing, there remains ethical choice. We choose the path of power or the path of love. Love is that path of openness to the universe which is our ultimate protection (from the madness of trying to micro manage life, if nothing else.) It is also the path through which the alternate realities of tenderness, kindness, ever growing wisdom, good will, joyful creative experience and expression, and healing are nurtured, shaped, and allowed to enter the world. If the world revels in ugliness as proof of intellectual superiority, we don't have to buy into it. We still can choose beauty, a beauty informed by connection to depth of spirit and nature that is our birthright. If the world is entertained by brutality, believing, as many do, that tenderness is weakness worthy only of mockery, and that the world consists of winners and losers, again, we don't have to buy into it. This is ethical choice.

There are those who wield might of arms and powerful bodies; there are those who wield finance; there are those who wield the power of the left-hand path, and there may well be those who wield all three. I will never be able to contend with them in their realms, for they are far more practiced at these things than I ever could be, (if for no other reason than that I find them boring) even if fear drove me to try, since those are not my paths. Mine is the path of the common people, the human birthright, even if it appears without hope that light can ultimately prevail in this very dark world. In fact, to live without hope is one of our oldest ethical teachings; that we did not begin this enterprise, nor will we finish it, but we may not desist from it. Nonetheless, I have a hope, and I will share it.

The Prophet Isaiah said, "The glory of the Lord shall be revealed and all flesh shall see it together." Whether or not the premise put forth in <u>The Hundredth Monkey</u> regarding a critical mass of consciousness has, in fact, been debunked (as I recall from somewhere it has) I can still operate out of a belief in the possibility of the world changing on the basis of an achievement of a critical mass of consciousness because, historically, it has. And even if it couldn't, it is my ethical responsibility to live as if it could. Thus we manifest the new reality.

I am not waiting for the Messiah. We are all responsible for striving to manifest messianic consciousness that ultimately is ethical responsibility both as individuals and community. I see Isaiah's prophesy as a description of a critical mass of consciousness. No, I don't believe it had to do particularly with our own times, but it is a principle that is applicable to any time.

It may well seem more powerful to carry a gun than to love a rainbow shining in the dew in a wild meadow.

It may well seem more powerful to take a curve at 80 miles per hour in a fancy sports car than to play the flute. It may well seem more powerful to blow up enemies than to make art or plant a garden, but if my power is to be one less person in the world who carries a gun, blows up buildings, and measures my worth by material possessions, then that is my power. My power is the prayer I pray for wisdom, healing, and ethical capacity in the world. It is a power that anyone alive can choose and maybe someday there will be enough people who make that choice. I may have to make that choice without any real hope, but it will have been an ethical choice nonetheless. Blessing is as real as cursing. In all deeds, thoughts and relationships we must ask, does this facilitate healing, creativity, mutuality, joyousness, and self-knowledge? Does this express kindness, protect the weak, contribute to the establishment of the foundations of liberty, respect, and clarity? Have we chosen an examined life or an unconscious one? Even with our best efforts, perfection certainly will not be achieved. But as the saying goes, "Wherever you go, there you are." In the face of the mockery of our smallness that efforts at goodness represent to some, we still must choose the good and seek to do so wisely because, on the level of spirit, we are creating the world in which we live.

The Myth of Spiritual Hierarchy

I would like to open my essay on the myth of spiritual hierarchy with two quotes from a book by Mel Levine, M..D. titled <u>The Myth of Laziness</u>.

". . . excessive social distractibility isn't confined to children. Social distractibility can obliterate output in adults, but sometimes the grown-up signs and symptoms are more subtle or insidious. I have had employees who seemed so consumed with their relationships with coworkers (some of whom they liked and respected and others of whom they loathed) that their social interactional issues became the overwhelming preoccupation within their chosen occupation.

I have encountered directly and heard about cases where output is compromised because such individuals are so distracted by their own need to build some relationships and perhaps undermine others. Obviously interactions in the workplace are of great importance, but not when they occupy such an elevated priority that they obscure the need to do a job efficiently. I was discussing this matter recently with the head of a large corporation. She identified this phenomenon as a major impediment to productivity. As she put it, "I have executives working for me who seem to exhaust themselves with their backroom gossip, their petty efforts to put down or victimize certain coworkers, their need to conspire against target victims, and their adolescent-like yearning to become part of a little gang of cool guys and dolls within the company. In the meantime, these social predators could be accomplishing so much more if they would only concentrate on their own creativity and productivity." P.163

"Our society cannot afford to neglect or remain unaware of output failure. We are paying an exorbitant price for the care of affected individuals as we subsidize their antidepressant medications, chronic unemployment, drug rehabilitation programs, and sometimes even incarceration." P. 167

Hierarchy is a fancy word for pecking order. Undoubtedly it is an efficient way of organizing a society, especially at the animal level. As can be seen from the above quotes, the application of pecking order, and the devious and cruel means by which it is enforced, to human societies also has an extremely detrimental aspect, (I can't, in fact, think of a job I have ever held, except when I was self-employed and working alone, including the last one I had for the seven and a half years before my retirement, where someone was not pulling this kind of crap on me) even more so when one has the belief system that projects these pecking orders onto the spiritual world.

It might do well here to offer my definition of the spiritual world. The spiritual world is the source of our freedom. It is pure love. It is the ground of our being. There is only one substance and one energy and they are One. I call this God or Creator, also Beloved and Holy One, Great Mystery. Others may be more comfortable with other names for this. That is their path to explore. This is the mystical view, how I experience it. Some people, who feel themselves to be on a spiritual path, recognizing the potential of oneness with the Divine, and the oneness of divine energy and substance, say that they <u>are</u> God. This may be technically accurate but it is definitely borderline. All that the individual is, is God, but the individual is far, far from being all of God that there is.

We place the spiritual above the physical on the one hand, yet say that intelligence is inherent in matter. Thus matter and spirit can be seen as one. Then we try to get around this by speaking of the refinement of matter into higher and higher spheres (from which such popular turns of phrase as "being on cloud nine" or "in seventh heaven" are derived.) Whole metaphysical systems have been developed out of this–Gnostic and Kabalistic, but I am not presently qualified to discuss those systems. Plenty of literature is available for those who have those interests.

From my point of view, there is no difference between the concept of a spiritual hierarchy and social Darwinism. There is no doubt that individuals have different capacities and abilities to be loving, wise, patient, understanding, of genuine good will, honest and open in communication and the development of social, artistic, and other mental skillfulness which is all the richer being informed by spirit. Indeed, one cannot reach true depth and height, true fullness of being, unless one does express spirit. But what does society value? We can complain that our caffeine-cocaine-meth-winner-take-all driven culture is not a spiritual culture, but when we claim the superiority of an oak over ants because of its longevity or hold the belief in a spiritual hierarchy, we are simultaneously buying into it and giving ourselves a consolation prize if we claim superiority on the basis of "spirituality."

Many are locked out of the economy by the greed

and power of a minority. On the other hand, children of privilege have grown up never having been kicked in the teeth despite their best efforts, so those who fail to make it are easily blamed for their plight in the name of "karma", or "weakness of will." They "just haven't got what it takes" to be the "cream which will rise."

Of course there are great arguments on both sides. Persons choosing, for example, pure organic, vegan diets, no use of drugs, getting a balanced amount of rest and healthful exercise, leading meditative and prayerful lives, taking responsibility for themselves, etc. can still get sick. Persons addicted to the adrenalin in flesh foods, smoking, drinking, and partying might live to be 98 and never be sick a day in their lives. Does this prove the superiority of the latter course? Such exceptions certainly provide people who choose that life style with plenty of excuses for not taking care of themselves. Who knows if they would have enjoyed life more or been more creative and humane without those lifestyle choices, those addictions to shallow insatiability? They might have lived to 120. As for the "perfect" person, they might live to be 58 as long as they take care of themselves when, if they failed to do so, they might have died at 30.

"Oh well that's just their karma working itself out."

I can hear some people saying. I think life is far too complex to be written off as karma. That's a simple (and dogmatic) explanation (excuse) for the fact that we do not understand much. Is there any explanation for the justice or injustice of life, of the world? (We all love "instant karma".) This is of course ultimately asking, "Why is there evil in the world." In all the centuries and eons of our existence we have tried and failed to fully answer this question. So this is just one more attempt to chip away at the "cosmic block."

The ground of a huge amount of evil in the world remains the concept of hierarchy. For wherever there is hierarchy, sooner or later there is enforcement of the presumed pecking order by violence or the threat of violence. Wherever there is enforcement, there is the repression of some aspect of spirit.

Does society need to have organizing principles? Certainly. Is the teacher/guru always wiser than the student? Not necessarily. Are men superior beings whose good karma allowed them to be born men and to whom all women should automatically give way? Well, we do know the answer to that one, don't we? Ahem. . . But I digress.

Once while I was still living at home, there was a

newspaper report about a young woman who was raped and thrown over a cliff in an attempted murder by the truck driver who had picked her up hitchhiking. The report said the girl may have been mildly retarded but went on to basically blame her because she had been hitchhiking. My mother said people who have such limitations deserve more protection, not less. That struck home in my mind as an absolute truth. We all struggle to balance judgment and compassion. We can all see instances when others should be more independent, more responsible for their lives, have more common sense, more capacity for logic, make more effort, when they should either put up or shut up. On the other hand, we have not walked in their path and we may remember times when we too were ignorant, were so tired, so despairing, so beat down, that we could not try any more. It is the responsibility of the more gifted to offer those in need of healing or guidance, aid in clarification of a positive path within their natural capacities, or at least a space where they can be facilitated in self-healing since we cannot always know the best way. When does someone need a swift kick in the pants to be forced to get on their feet to take care of themselves when they are, in fact, able, and when do they need simple respect and hearing? If one would engage in helping, you had better have some measure of a concept regarding this, because judgment can place a stumbling block in front of the blind.

What is real, the physical or the spiritual? What is "superior", the philanthropist or the criminal, the rich or the poor? What is the purpose of our being? Does the concept of karma and reincarnation lead to the spiritual equivalent of laissez fair or a genuine concern for justice; i.e., improvement of human circumstances, working to change the cultural structure of judgment that writes people off rather than say, early intervention for troubled families, special education, recognition of difference and individuality in learning style and temperament. What is hell? For the extrovert, lack of outside stimulation. For the introvert, too much outside stimulation. Clearly we need individualized education rather than the waste of factory-style mass education that allows so many to fall by the wayside as "stupid" and "worthless" "failures" and "losers." (Up to 33 percent of young people drop out of high school and it is 80 percent of these that wind up in our jails.) When will we turn from the triumphalism that equates health and wealth with goodness (or good karma) and poverty with evil and/or failure, or even "justice", as if we were still parading about in puritanical garb?

I may say at this point that I have pretty strong, if subjective, evidence that reincarnation is an actuality though I am not going to go into that now. If karma is a reality, however, it is not personal. Our thoughts and deeds are a part of the ongoing creation of the world. To the degree that we create goodness and facilitate light in the world, we may come to it in succeeding incarnations, so also with the darkness we create. And bringing soul habits into succeeding incarnations may incline us to wind up with circumstances and environments that cause the consequences of those habits to manifest. Any idea of punishment and reward, however, I think is better left to priesthoods that seek to control people with fears of heaven and hell. Gandhi said, "Be the change you want to see." I think this is what Jesus meant when he said, "The Kingdom of heaven is within you."

For better or worse, one seeks wisdom and strives to manifest the good and to find the ways to grow in those capacities. I can say honestly that I have a great amount of bitterness in this life as well as many gifts and blessings. Despite the bitterness, the soul habit I strive to cultivate is gratitude and blessing.

We cannot say that the universe is spiritual, i.e. that

intelligence exists inherent in matter, and also say that physiology and outward circumstances are not factors in life's outcomes, dogmatically blaming people for their illness rather than recognizing when a polluted environment has overwhelmed the immune system or our genes. Nor can the perpetrators of genocide or other crimes be exonerated by some fantasy about the evil or worthlessness of the victim, as in, "you were raped because your skirt was too short." The Holocaust happened because of the widespread European belief that Jews killed Jesus. This is a historical lie, (Roman propaganda actually) but it spawned a belief system that resulted in mass murder and torture of millions. We are responsible to think out the consequences of our belief systems.

White settlers had the belief that land should be used for farming and ranching so felt justified in taking Native American land because native peoples were hunter gatherers. (They were also farmers, as may be witnessed by the fact that half of present world food crops were, in fact, developed in the Americas, but they weren't white so it didn't matter.)

And what about the school yard? Bullying is seen in many cultures as a severe problem that carries on in adult life (see opening quotes.) Yet adult society continues to be scarred by just such behavior and many children are crushed in spirit. When the bully says they're going to knock somebody's lights out, it is said and done on a spiritual level as well as the physical, whether the bully has any clue regarding spirituality or not. Our culture, on the level of hideous hubris, now lauds more than ever the "winner", the one who crushes all opposition. We are stuck in an adversarial win/lose, one up/one down outlook that has no room for win/win. It can't even conceive of any other way of looking at life as it spawns argument for sport rather than principle, and triumphal crushing of the light of anyone who is seen as a threat, especially if another is more creative, intelligent, or gentle, or a member of a feared class. It is a philosophy that says, don't try to improve yourself through relationship, be open to learning from them, share what you have joyously–just crush them. You'll be the winner which certainly proves you're superior. Envy and jealousy grow from feelings of inadequacy which grow from the cultural emphasis on competitiveness, which sells a lot of products since everybody has to have IT and IT keeps changing with the marketplace consumer treadmill.

Culture is the sum total of our belief systems. Can we have a culture in which it is recognized that we are deeply related, that the very atomic structure of matter is relationship, not isolation? Not if we believe in hierarchy which must be enforced by bullying and wining, as hierarchy must, because it is against nature, unless of course you are either a social Darwinist or simply cannot see a need to outgrow primate behavior if we are to become fully human.

There are two ways in which a culture can operate smoothly. One based on fear (hierarchy) and one based on respect (equality.) Bullying is inherent in any system of hierarchy for, to have a hierarchy, the individuality of some (designated Other/losers) and their spontaneity, creativity, joyousness must be repressed. This leads to much bitterness on the part of those repressed and much loss of their offering and the fruit of their offering, both to themselves and the wider society. The purpose of bullying is always to establish hierarchy or, to clarify its basis in animal behavior, pecking order. These two systems have been at war with one another for at least ten thousand years.

The primary representative of a hierarchical system, or rather the one we in the West are most aware of is, of course, Rome. Two more egalitarian systems, out of which we still derive much richness and alternative thinking, were the Celtic and the Jewish (though the Celts too, being Indo-European had a cast system similar to that of the Hindus) The cast system of India is another hierarchy ultimately derived from the same proto culture that moved both east and west out of the steppes of central Asia and Persia (Iran). It may be argued that Judaism too was hierarchic. It was, after all, a part of the same great migration of peoples, ultimately due to long-term cycles of climate change in Asia (see <u>The Mummies of Urumchie by Elizabeth Barber</u>.)

In the Bible we see that the destruction of native peoples (Canaanites) was ordered. But Judaism is an integration of many factors, including the Canaanite, and the Prophet's call for justice and the proto-democracy, of the proclamation that <u>all</u> were children of God, was a command for respect and equality (and which parallels the Egyptian democratization of the afterlife from a state of existence which only royalty could attain to one in which, slowly but surely, lower ranks were admitted as reflected by their mummification practices.) Women in both Celtic and early Jewish society participated in the religious and political life of the people though the Celtic society was far more extensive. In Rome women were seen to be useful only for their reproductive capacities and as objects of pleasure.

The concept of time being of war or peace bears some reflection here. War time is speed time (war, the ultimate contest of bullies) no time for thought or the creation of consensus. Peace time is respect time. Genuine peace produces and is produced by communion and consensus, by taking time. Respect and honor are born of the essentially democratic ideal of all being children of God and the slowing down of time to look, think, reflect, sense, experience the contours and potential of shared creative endeavor (culture) and draw out the consequences of action (in short, to brainstorm) to the seventh generation. This is an attitude which says I will listen to you. I will honor you. I will give weight to your words and deeds. I will give space to your work and thought so that they may flower and be part of the shared beauty of the world. We will have time to deeply know and understand and support one another and we would do so out of the joy of mutual honor, and curiosity in sharing, discovering, and exploring life and each other.

Absent both respect and curiosity we have the society we today live in that is going down the tubes. Cruelty prevails because that is the shortcut to hierarchic power. The meanest wins. Wins what? A radioactive hoard of clutter, living in the belief that what you have is what you are and for which one is willing to kill at all levels. Ah, the glamorous hoard, the trophy lover, the hyper flow of shallow entertainment for the insatiable, all plugged in to the media that is owned by the powers who profit from the rampant consumerism, the hyper competitiveness that sends everyone to the mall to buy compensation for their sense of inadequacy, the discount of anything that smacks of opposition to this mindlessness. If it is mindless, it is tabula rasa, easily to manipulate your every resource into their pocket. So we have a culture that can say, "Nuke 'em," if that's what we need to feel secure with our bloody hoard. We are the top of the hierarchy after all, we're the best in the world, so it doesn't matter what we do. We're the winners.

Well, we have nuked 'em. Depleted uranium weapons that aerosolize into radioactive particles smaller than viruses that will be producing cancers and birth defects for the next nine billion years in every living being they lodge in have been spewed all over the middle east (Iraq, Kuwait) and Europe (Kosovo) and everywhere American soldiers are stationed. They too are exposed to this now omnipresent radioactive dust. The hierarchy is intact. Presently in Iraq they know who's the boss. The interpreters are being sent out to get chicken and sodas.

Hierarchy: Some believe everything must be viewed in terms of it. The oak then is to be accounted superior to the ant because of its longevity. What if the ant has superiority because of its mobility and the oak is stuck where it grows and cannot escape the ax? Ah, but that is the karma and place of the oak, to yield to the one who wields the ax, for that one is obviously superior. But the oak produces food for all with its acorns and what superiority does the one cutting the tree have if his intent is to use the wood to burn or crucify someone? Only evil failures suffer from the bad karma of a lowly incarnation as what? An ant instead of an oak? A woman instead of a man? A slave instead of a whip wielder? A quadriplegic instead of an athlete? Some are worthy of their seventeen Cadillacs while others can barely keep one car running well enough to get them to a job to which they may go despite arthritic hands and bad backs so as not to burden others with their care? Some need not work at all while others are expected to lick their toes? Then there is no need to strive for justice. That's easy. Let's the grand winners off the hook for all their actions.

They're superior or they wouldn't have achieved such positions of privilege. ("And damned are them that dare resist or touch the Lord's anointed.") Right? Bronx cheer.

No need to think about what mockery, bullying, violence and threats do the spirits of those on the receiving end. They deserve what they get or they wouldn't be getting it. Must have been real evil folks in some previous life time. Tell that to the victims of the Nazis. Tell that to the Native Americans. You tell it to the women and children beaten into submission and silence by the relentless enforcement of men's superior place. Tell it to the spirits of the trees in the clear-cut. Tell it to the babies born with hands growing out of their shoulders because their fathers were exposed to depleted uranium dropped on them by the country with good karma while their country must be massively guilty of <u>something</u>. Tell it to the street children in South American slums who have their eyes gouged out by drug dealers because they saw too much. Tell it to the people who drowned in the floods of Bangladesh. Tell it to the women of Afghanistan who were beaten if they went out and showed so much as an elbow, who could not work even when widowed but had to beg for food. Tell it to the victims of torture. Tell it to the little girls in Africa who have their clitoris cut off with tin can lids and no anesthetic and their labia sewn shut in order to insure their faithfulness and virginity as wives. Tell it to all the people who have AIDS, including the ones who got it from blood transfusions. Tell it to the people buried under mud slides when multinationals clear cut the hills above their villages. Tell it to the kitten thrown live onto a barbeque. Tell it to the horse ridden by a sadistic teenage girl into freezing water and forced to stand there up to its belly. Oh, you have bad karma. Tell it to the child whose legs and butt are given third-degree burns because its mother sat it on a stove for peeing in its pants. Tell it to the 150,000 to three million women (exact number remains unknown but the lower figure is certain) who were burned at the stake as witches over a period of three hundred years while their daughters were forced to watch. Tell it to the Iraqi boy who had both his arms blown off by American bombs. Tell it to the little boy raped by his mother's boyfriend in the bed he was forced to share with them. Tell it to the women of Congo as they are devastated by the current civil war and the rule of the gun. Tell it to the child soldiers kidnapped and forced to kill or be killed, forever alienated from their villages.

Tell it to the victims of snuff films. Tell it to the children fleeing from physical and sexual abuse at home to lives of hell on the streets because they have nowhere to go. Tell it to the napalmed children in Viet Nam. Oh, what bad karma you have.

The idea of karma is for the privileged and the lucky. Hierarchy, spiritual or otherwise, is nothing but an excuse for all the bullying required to enforce it. And all, all these things have been based on a hierarchical view of the world, the "superiority" of the one who can get away with whatever he/she damn well pleases, the ones who have no empathy. Behold the consequences of the philosophy that hierarchy is essential reality, the world exactly as it is.

We wish to know how the world has come to be in such a state, somehow to draw security around us. Something, someone must be in control. Hierarchy provides the delusion of security as well as the fruits of the labor of others for those who have privilege, hence they cling to it.

But in truth, we must live with the mystery and the unbearable tension of paradox. Our love must become expansive to the point of transparency, open to the universe. There will never be any ultimate security but that.

A CONDENSED HISTORY OF THE COLD WAR

The U.S. hired Nazis to spy on the Russians after WWII. This set the tone of American anti-communism. For documentation of earlier U.S. collaboration with Nazis, suggested reading is <u>Trading With The Enemy</u>, <u>The Nazi-American Money Plot</u> by Charles Higham. This is out of print but available from second-hand book dealers.

Claus Barbie, the Butcher of Lyons, was one of these. U.S. assisted his escape to Bolivia rather than turn him over to France, as originally promised, when his spy work was finished.

1947 Truman signs National Security Act establishing the security state– CIA. Suggested reading, <u>Journey Into Madness</u> by Gordon Thomas.

1953 Mohammed Masaddeq, popular and legitimately elected president of Iran, nationalized Iran's oil fields. U.S. outraged. English no longer permitted to profit from them. CIA paid mobs to beat up any citizens who did not have a photo of the Shaw on their cars. These mobs returned the Shaw to power. SAVAK–CIA created the Shah's secret police who tortured and murdered thousands of the Shaw's opponents.

1954 "Concepts of fair play no longer apply." Hoover

1979   Iranian uprising ousted the Shaw and put in Ayatollah Khomeini.

1986   Iran-Contra, Nicaragua. "Freedom Fighters." Reagan vows to be "tough on terrorists" "no concessions." Weapons for hostages deal made. Israel a key player in sale of arms to Iran for release of hostages in Lebanon. Profits from arms sales fund Contras in Nicaragua. Contras entirely CIA funded, based in Guatemala, fought guerilla war against legitimately elected Sandinista government. 100,000 peasants died. Albet Hakim brokered missile sales to Iran at a huge profit to the CIA–$10 million. Iranian attacks on Iraq with these missiles killed one million people.

Iraq supplied by multinationals (chemical and pharmaceutical companies) in both U.S. and Europe with all the components for building his war machine with unconventional weapons. Many Iranians dead.

Suggested reading, <u>The Eleventh Plague</u>.

1960   Guatemala–Legitimately elected president Hakabo Arbenz, U.S. ally, often voting with U.S. in the United Nations, nationalized land, including his own, and gave to peasants to correct situation of 3%

of population owning 70% of the land. This was intolerable to a U.S. company – United Fruit – who were determined to keep Guatemala a "banana republic." This so tainted the name of United Fruit they had to change their name to Chiquita. Honduran mercenaries hired, operated as death squads resulted in 100,000 deaths under U.S. backed military dictatorships over 30-year period. Land returned to original owners, United Fruit.

1961 Bay of Pigs invasion.

1967 CIA turns to the Mafia for help in attempts to overthrow Castro. Castro hated because of his success in throwing out U.S. backed dictator Batista.

1968 VIET NAM CIA in 1954 set up puppet regime of Diem shortly after independence won from France. Kennedy sent 15,000 Green Beret "advisers." Gulf of Tonkin incident not unprovoked. Intelligence warned it would happen. This gave Johnson a blank check for massive build-up of American forces.

LAOS "belongs to the CIA." Recruitment of Hmong and Lao hill tribes to fight Viet Cong. U.S. armed them and abandoned them. Many are now living on welfare in

American cities.

Fifty eight thousand U.S. troops died in Viet Nam.

AFGHANISTAN CIA funded mujahidin in proxy war against Soviets. Some of this money funneled to what later became Al Qaeda.

CHILE Legitimately elected president Allende overthrown by CIA. Military dictatorship of Pinochet established. Death squads and torture ensue. Attempts to bring Pinochet to trial in Chile ongoing until recently.

A FEW AMERICAN INVENTIONS

Germ warfare research (also engaged in by Russia) began at the end of WWII. U.S. populations in New York received doses of illness causing but non-lethal bacteria (light bulbs painted black and filled with these pathogens were thrown onto subway tracks) in secret experiments to see how agents spread. Many became ill. (See <u>The Eleventh Plague</u>)
Nuclear weapons have actually been used by only one country, the U.S.

Napalm–extensively used in Viet Nam–jellied gasoline clings to skin, courtesy of Dow Chemical Company. Same chemical additive that makes cling wrap cling.

FURTHER RECOMMENDED READING

<u>Deadly Deceits</u> by Frank Magee

<u>The 11th Plague: The Politics of Chemical and Biological Warfare</u> by Leonard Cole

<u>The Argument Culture</u> by Debora Tannen

As we live in a so-called democracy, where the citizens have responsibility to correct the errors of their government, this kind of history must be neither ignored nor justified. We have the responsibility to educate ourselves regarding the actions of our government and to do our best to see that life is respected. The above history proves that respect for either democracy or human life has only been given lip service and thousands of deaths have resulted.

I don't give a damn if it is the great, wonderful, "democratic," peace-loving, heroic, chosen Americans who are responsible or not. IT IS WRONG. IT IS VILE. IT IS STUPID. IT IS EVIL.

ABOUT THE AUTHOR

Naomi Silvertree (aka Margo Gross) was born in California. She moved with her parents at the age of six months, to a 12' by 14' cabin on Little Lake Road, just outside of Mendocino and attended public schools there. Now retired, she maintains an interest in the study of history, religion, psychology, music, art, and folk lore. She is also an avid gardener and folk dancer.